Editor
Walter Kelly, M.A.

Managing Editor
Elizabeth Morris, Ph.D.

Illustrator
Kevin McCarthy

Cover Artist
Brenda DiAntonis

Art Manager
Kevin Barnes

Art Director
CJae Froshay

Imaging
Richard E. Easley
Rosa C. See

Publisher
Mary D. Smith, M.S. Ed.

- Traits of Good Writing
- The Writing Process
- Parts of Speech
- Editing & Publishing
- Writers Workshop
- Brainstorming

Author

Jennifer Overend Pri...

Teacher Created Resources, Inc.
6421 Industry Way
Westminster, CA 92683
www.teachercreated.com

©2005 Teacher Created Resources, Inc.
Made in U.S.A.
ISBN-1-4206-3379-1

Table of Contents

Introduction 3

The Writing Environment 8

**Part I: Teacher's Guides and
Student Pages** 14

Storytelling 15

Journal Writing 19

Phonemic Awareness Activities 28

Group Writing Experiences 38

Sentence Writing 45

Story Writing 54

Writing Traits: Ideas and Content 56

Writing Traits: Organization 64

Writing Traits: Voice 75

Writing Traits: Word Choice 79

Writing Traits: Sentence Fluency 88

Writing Traits: Conventions 92

Writing Traits: Presentation 104

Writing Traits in Literature 124

Word Play: Idioms 125

Word Play: Similes 126

Word Play: Onomatopoeia 126

Word Play: Personification 127

Word Play: Hink Pinks 127

Word Play: Alliteration 128

Word Play: Imagery 128

Songwriting 146

Extending Vocabulary 150

Letter Writing 152

Book Reports 166

Simple Research Report 172

Poetry: Creating Rhymes 177

Poetry: Couplets 177

Poetry: Cinquain 177

Poetry: Shape Poems, I Feel Poems,
Name Poems 178

Poetry: Haiku 179

Descriptive Writing 187

Expository Writing 199

Persuasive and Narrative Writing 202

Checking for Spelling 206

Assessment 216

Part II: Writer's Notebook 225

Writing Process Checklist 226

Brainstorming Topics 227

My Memoirs 228

"Said" Words 229

Self-Assessment Checklist 230

Synonyms 231

Homophones 232

Similes 233

Idioms 234

Onomatopoeia 235

Friendly Letter Template 236

Business Letter Template 237

Letter Writing Greetings 238

Addressing an Envelope:
State Abbreviations 239

Writing a News Article 240

Writing a Book Report 241

Proofreading Symbols 242

Poetry Templates 243

Word Families 247

Adjectives 250

Synonyms for Emotions 251

Story Structure 252

Character Description 253

Answer Key 254

References 255

Introduction

The *Jumbo Book of Writing Lessons* is designed to be used as a perpetual reference for all major writing skills necessary to become a good writer. This book is divided into two parts.

Part I

This section of the book contains lessons designed to guide students through the following writing topics:

- ❏ writing process/writers workshop
- ❏ the writing environment
- ❏ traits of good writing
    - ideas
    - organization
    - voice
    - word choice
    - sentence fluency
    - conventions
    - methods of presentation
- ❏ parts of speech
- ❏ nouns
- ❏ adjectives
- ❏ verbs
- ❏ high-frequency words
- ❏ similes
- ❏ metaphors
- ❏ onomatopoeia
- ❏ synonyms
- ❏ antonyms
- ❏ idioms
- ❏ alliteration
- ❏ personification
- ❏ friendly letters
- ❏ business letters
- ❏ opinions/editorials
- ❏ book report
- ❏ news article
- ❏ poetry (different kinds, include rhyming)
- ❏ writing domains (descriptive, expository, narrative, persuasive)
- ❏ editing
- ❏ publishing
- ❏ mini-books
- ❏ story prompts

Each lesson begins with a Teacher's Guide page that sets the stage for the accompanying student pages. Space for additional teacher ideas or comments is provided on many teacher pages.

The lessons and reproducibles developed in Part I should be implemented to reinforce, as well as to supplement, pages in the Writer's Notebook (Part II). Part I includes a number of writing prompt pages for additional writing practice.

Part II

This section is referred to as the Writer's Notebook. It contains examples, forms, rules, and other helpful information that support and reinforce the lessons in Part I. Writer's Notebook pages should be distributed to the students as personal references for writing skills. Students can keep their notebooks with them in the classroom and use them for homework assignments.

What Is the Writing Process?

The writing process is a natural procedure used by professional writers. It involves preparatory writing tasks, drafting, peer response, editing, revising, and publishing. These steps should be imitated by student writers since they dramatically improve the quality of completed writings. The steps are outlined below, and a student copy of the process can be found on page 226 of the Writer's Notebook. On page 14 a teacher's copy of the process approach appears in poster form to open the Teacher's Guide section.

Brainstorming

Brainstorming is the first step in the writing process. It involves thinking of all the ideas you can about a topic. You list the ideas on chart paper or on a chalkboard for all to see. All children sit at a meeting place and take turns sharing their ideas. In this book, you'll find many activities that involve the beginning step of brainstorming before writing.

Writing

Writing is the next step in the writing process. After you make a chart of all the ideas about a subject, the children select one or more ideas about which to write a few sentences or a whole story. Young children can copy words from the brainstorming list and then think of something to write about the topic. Encourage invented spelling for beginning writers. This book provides numerous opportunities for the writing stage, including the following elements:

- organization
- voice
- fluency
- story prompts

- writing genres
- poetry writing
- letter writing
- news article writing

Introduction *(cont.)*

Editing/Revising

Editing/revising is the next step in the writing process. The children read their sentences to themselves and then to partners. They check to see if the sentences or stories make sense and if they have written everything they want to say. (Depending on the age and skill of the children, you can have them work on revising, in addition to editing, to focus more on clarity and description, rather than on writing conventions.) If the children need help, they ask a friend or an adult. They also check for correct punctuation as part of the editing. In this book, you'll find activities for the following elements:

- conventions
- editing
- revising
- publishing

Recopying

This is writing a final, edited draft of a story. Keep in mind that this step is often omitted for very young children as they will focus mostly on the brainstorming and writing stages.

Publishing

This important step can take many forms, including illustrating, bookbinding, word-processing, layout and graphics, displays, publications, group sharing, or performances. This is a vital set of interconnected activities which enable children to display their work in creative ways.

What Are the Traits of Good Writing?

A model for emphasizing the traits of good writing is fast becoming a popular instructional method in the country. This approach developed as teachers expressed an interest in more direction for the instruction of writing. They wanted to have a common language concerning writing to use with students, parents, and the community. They also wanted a systematic, analytical scoring system that could be used when evaluating students' writing.

As this system developed, several writing traits emerged that define children's writing:

- ❑ ideas
- ❑ organization
- ❑ voice
- ❑ word choice
- ❑ sentence fluency
- ❑ conventions

The goal of this approach is not necessarily to focus on all of the traits at one time or even to focus on all of them at each grade level. This is merely a model of writing assessment that defines the qualities of good writing.

Defining the Traits of Good Writing

❑ **Ideas**

Ideas refer to the content of the writing. The focus is on clear messages, use of detail, and presentation of information.

❑ **Organization**

Organization refers to the structure of the writing. The focus is on logical sequence of events and strong connections made between parts of the story.

❑ **Voice**

Voice refers to the voice of the writer coming through in the writing. It gives the story feeling and individuality.

❑ **Word Choice**

The word choice trait focuses on the use of rich language and descriptive writing to impress or move the reader.

❑ **Sentence Fluency**

Sentence fluency refers to the rhythm and flow of the writing. Fluent writing is pleasing to the ear and allows the reader's thoughts to flow freely with the story.

❑ **Conventions**

Conventions refer to the mechanics of the written work. The focus is on spelling, grammar, use of paragraphs, use of capital letters, and punctuation.

❑ **Presentation**

Presentation focuses on the visual elements of the writing. This can refer to handwriting, neatness, format, or use of visual aids.

Why Teach the Traits of Writing?

The writing traits apply to a variety of writing styles and purposes. Mastery of the traits gives students the writing skills they will use throughout their lives. Teachers need a variety of resources to help them support students in their journey toward becoming good writers. Look in any teacher's library and you will find many, many books about teaching writing. No single method of teaching is going to be a quick solution to problems in writing, but focusing on the traits of writing will allow you and your students to concentrate on one element of writing at a time. This breaks the task of learning to write effectively into manageable parts.

The Writing Environment

During the early years, children show rapid development of writing skills, which is why it is so important for young children to experience language through opportunities to read, write, listen, and speak. Kindergarteners and preschoolers tend to be more interested in the writing itself, but as they mature, children tend to become interested in the final product. Communicate to parents the stages of writing (Sulzby, 1985), by duplicating page 10 and sending it home. You might want to discuss these writing stages at a parent night or at conferences to increase parent understanding and address questions. There are many ways to create an environment that is conducive to writing development.

The Literacy Center

Providing a literacy center in your classroom develops positive attitudes toward reading and writing and encourages children to enjoy and experiment with language and literature.

Your literacy center should be a focal point of your classroom. Partition the area on two sides with bookshelves, file cabinets, or freestanding bulletin boards. The center should have bookshelves to hold literature and reference books. It is also helpful to have a display shelf for featured books. Create a comfortable setting in the center by providing cushions, beanbag chairs, or an area rug. You'll also want to provide a table and chairs for the writing area. Adorn the walls of the center with writing- and literature-related posters. You may want to have your classroom computer in this area for word-processing. Make the area inviting. Provide a variety of writing materials and resources. Encourage the writing of new words, stories, books, cards, advertisements, etc. Here's a list of materials you can include in your literacy center.

Literacy Center Materials

- children's books
- tape recorder
- paper (in all sizes and colors)
- poster board or tagboard
- stationery and envelopes
- pencils and pens
- colored markers
- scissors
- glue

- index cards
- stamps and a stamp pad
- stencils
- construction paper
- stapler
- hole puncher
- magazines and newspapers
- environmental print (product boxes, fast-food bags, etc.)

Your literacy center should be a place of endless possibilities. In addition to reading and writing creatively, your children should be encouraged to use functional writing. Functional writing is writing with a purpose. Forms of functional writing include greeting cards, notes, messages, thank-you cards, lists, address books, telephone books, advertisements, mail (even junk mail), message boards, and more.

The Literacy Center *(cont.)*

You can encourage the use of functional writing in a variety of ways. Have your children do the following:

- write birthday cards
- write thank-you letters
- make supply lists or "to do" lists
- make a list of favorite TV shows
- write letters to pen pals
- post messages on a class message board

Be sure to draw children's attention to examples of functional print in your classroom. Bring in junk mail and advertisements to show. Encourage the children to look for functional print in and around the home.

Independent Writing

In order to become proficient writers, it is important for your children to have plenty of time to write independently. Your children may enjoy writing about the following:

- a familiar book character
- questions that they have
- something that interests them
- something that happened in their lives
- what makes them curious
- what makes them sad
- what makes them angry

Independent writing time should be a time for exploration and enthusiasm. Encourage creativity and focus on personal interests.

Ways to Practice Writing

There are numerous ways to have children practice writing in very informal ways. Participating in informal writing tasks communicates to students that writing is a part of our everyday lives. Page 11 provides a list of informal writing ideas for you to use with your students. You'll also find a page (page 227) in the Writer's Notebook where students have the chance to create their own list of writing ideas.

Children's Literature and Writing

There is a strong connection between children's literature and writing. Through literature, your children are exposed to creative language and interesting story lines. The use of predictable books provides exposure to language patterns that they can imitate in their writing. Children's literature can inspire your children to write stories about characters they know or create new ones. They can be inspired to write about adventures or about personal experiences. There are numerous Web sites that offer read-aloud suggestions for young children, such as Carol Hurst's Children's Literature Site (*http://www.carolhurst.com*). Be sure to click on Featured Books to find book reviews and lists of reading and writing extensions.

Home Writing Ideas

Enhance your students' writing skills by encouraging reinforcement from home. Duplicate the home writing ideas on pages 11–12 and send home to parents.

Stages of Writing Development

Sulzby (1985) identifies six stages of writing development.

1. **Writing via drawing.**

   The child uses drawing to convey messages.

2. **Writing via scribbling.**

   The child makes scribbles from left to right with the intention of conveying a message.

3. **Writing via making letter-like forms.**

   The child's scribbles begin to look like letters. The letters tend to be made up by the child.

4. **Writing via reproducing well-learned units or letter strings.**

   The child begins to use familiar strings of letters. For example, the child may use the letters in his or her name, but may change the order of some of the letters. Letters may also appear in long strings with random order.

5. **Writing via invented spelling.**

   The child begins to write, using his or her own creations for words not known. A single letter might represent an entire word or syllable.

6. **Writing via conventional spelling.**

   The child begins to write in a form that begins to resemble adult writing.

Ways to Practice Writing

The following is a list of areas where writing is used. Ask your students to brainstorm a similar list for themselves (see page 226 of the Writer's Notebook). Use the list to help you create a variety of writing assignments.

- postcards
- letters
- invitations
- cartoons
- newspaper articles
- newspaper ads
- flyers
- pop-up books
- sentence frames
- poetry
- notes
- lists
- book reports
- interviews
- autobiographies
- biographies
- family histories
- folktales
- commercials
- labels
- journals
- diaries
- photo or postcard captions
- menus
- daily bulletins/news
- jokes
- riddles

- bumper stickers
- questions
- recipes
- directions
- story summaries
- announcements
- schedules
- phone messages
- word lists
- greeting cards
- graphic organizers
- story mapping
- sticky notes
- letterheads
- business cards
- mottoes
- billboards
- name tags
- thank-you notes
- shape books
- reminder notes
- fairy tales
- character descriptions
- gift tags
- addressing envelopes
- weather reports

Home Writing Ideas

Family Stories

Children's stories are often based on real-life experiences and/or family members. You can assist your child with story ideas by telling true stories of family members and memorable events. Share your own childhood stories, describe your hometown, tell stories about a favorite pet, etc. In turn, invite your child to tell stories of favorite memories.

Vacation Journal

Journaling on a family vacation is a great way to inspire writing ideas. Purchase or assemble a special book just for the occasion and explain to your child that he or she will have the opportunity to document the events of the trip. This will not only help your child to practice writing skills, but will also preserve family memories for years to come.

Parent Notes to Child

Encourage your child's writing by example. On a daily or weekly basis, write a simple note to your child. This might be a reminder note or a note telling about his or her special qualities. You'll likely find that your child will begin writing notes to you in return.

Newspaper Articles

Select a newspaper article that you think your child would enjoy. Read the article aloud together. Then you may work together to write a summary of the news story.

Personal Journal

Encourage your child to keep a daily journal to record events of the day, questions, and feelings. Discuss topics to address in the journal and allow your child to read particular entries to you if he or she so chooses.

Story Characters

Discuss with your child story characters that have become favorites. Then think about other storylines for the character and how he or she might handle them. Ask your child to dictate a new storyline with the favorite character as you write your child's words on paper. Reread the new story together.

Letter Writing

Begin a routine of letter writing with your child. This is a great way for him or her to stay in touch with faraway relatives or friends. Be sure to discuss the format of a friendly letter as the two of you construct the letters together. You might also want to encourage the writing of thank-you notes, reminder notes, and postcards.

Home Writing Ideas *(cont.)*

Keep on Reading

It is important to know that reading and writing are strongly connected and that children need to hear read-aloud selections from proficient readers in order to improve their own reading and writing skills. So, take frequent trips to the library and make daily read-aloud time a routine in your family.

Writing Discussions

As you and your child participate in shared writing experiences, discuss its many uses. Draw attention to the ways we use writing every day, such as in the following activities:

- sending e-mail
- making lists
- writing letters or memos
- recording events on a calendar
- taking telephone messages
- doing homework
- completing applications
- writing notes to friends
- keeping journals

Family Announcements

Display a family message board in a prominent location of your home. Encourage the whole family to check the board daily for messages and to write down messages they have to share.

E-mail

Encourage your child to write letters to friends and family by sending e-mail. Explain that it is still important to check for spelling, capitalization, and punctuation when sending messages electronically. (Be sure to monitor your child's Internet use to ensure his or her safety.)

Connecting Writing and Art

If your child loves to draw, encourage him or her to create a book of these artistic creations. Create a booklet by stapling together several sheets of construction paper. Then paste a drawing onto each page. Be sure to have your child create a decorative cover, complete with his or her name, and the book's title. Ask your child to write a brief description of each drawing.

Remember that routine writing experiences at home support writing experiences in school. You'll find that your child takes enjoyment in the process and that his or her skills will improve over time.

Part I

Teacher's Guides

and

Student Pages

The Process Approach

1. **Prewriting:** This is the stage where children generate ideas for writing. This stage involves brainstorming, reading, creating story maps, making word banks, etc.

2. **Rough Draft:** The rough draft stage is where the children put their ideas on paper. The focus is not on writing conventions or neatness, but on the story itself.

3. **Reread:** In this stage, the children read their stories aloud to make sure they have written clearly.

4. **Share with a Peer Revisor:** This stage involves sharing written work with a classmate who makes suggestions for change or improvement. The peer revisor asks questions about the story and seeks clarification from the author.

5. **Revise:** The revision stage involves improving the written work by adding details, interesting language, and suggestions from the peer revisor.

6. **Editing:** This stage involves children working together to correct errors in mechanics and spelling.

7. **Final Draft:** Children write their final copies, discussing revisions with the teacher.

8. **Publishing:** The final stage allows children to publish their stories by making books, placing them on display, or reading them aloud.

(**Teacher Note:** Duplicate this poster for classroom display.)

Storytelling

Even though we expect that our students' writing will improve over time and that we can offer ways to assist them in this process, remember to enjoy their early stages of writing just the way they are. The more students' writing is read and valued and understood, the more motivated they will be to continue to experiment with writing. You can assist your children with developing ideas and improving their writing ability by having them participate in prewriting activities, such as storytelling.

Before you begin preparing activities for writing instruction, it is important that your children understand that they have stories to tell.

At the beginning of every day, after attendance, and lunch count, and all of the morning routine, allow your students to tell stories. Keep this time informal. Begin by saying, "Does anyone have anything to share?" Stress the importance of listening. This will take a little bit of time, but the children will soon realize that they will all have their chance to tell a story and that everyone will listen to them when they do. Inevitably, you will see that one story leads to another and another on the same topic.

This is a wonderful way to watch the children as they wait to hear their classmates' stories. Rather than waiting to tell their own stories, they'll begin to enjoy playing off the stories of others. The purpose of this is so that all children will realize they have stories to tell—stories that are interesting, worth listening to, and worth writing about.

Storytelling does not always have to be about personal experiences. Learning to orally create stories is a valuable skill as well.

Learn more about storytelling by performing an Internet search on the topic. You're sure to find many useful Web sites that will provide more insight and ideas for storytelling with young children. Here are some ideas to get started with storytelling in your classroom.

Retelling Fairy Tales

Group students into pairs and have them take turns retelling favorite fairy tales.

Encourage the children to think about the characters in the tale and include details describing the characters and events that take place in the story.

Picture This

1. Select a photograph or painting to show the children.

2. Ask the children to think about the story they think the image tells.

3. Encourage them to offer their ideas.

4. Then determine a general idea for the story and ask the children to dictate sentences to tell the story as you write their words on chart paper.

5. Pictures are provided on pages 17 and 18 for you to use for story inspiration.

Storytelling Planner

Use this page to plan a story you will tell aloud to the class or a friend.

Is this story exciting, interesting, scary, etc.?

_____

_____

Why do you want to share this story?

_____

_____

Who is in the story?

_____

_____

When did this happen?

_____

_____

What happened first?

_____

_____

_____

_____

What happened next?

_____

_____

How did the story end?

_____

_____

Practice telling the story out loud before sharing it with the class. Use your notes on this page to help you tell the story.

Picture This

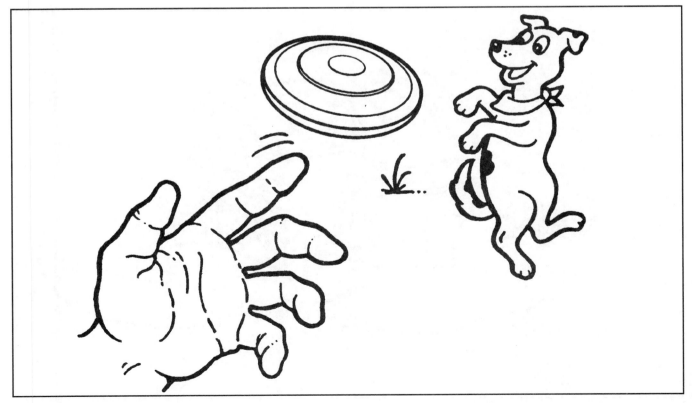

Picture This

Journal Writing

Traditional journal writing can be used daily or several times a week to allow children to write at their own developmental levels. Initially, journaling might include scribbles or drawings, which will eventually lead to the use of invented spelling and then more conventional spelling.

Journaling can take on a dialogue format where the teacher responds to the child's writing with a comment or a question. The use of dialogue can help the child expand on his or her written descriptions.

Journal writing in your classroom can take on many forms. You may need to vary your journaling routine from year to year, depending on the interests and needs of your students.

Dialogue journaling is a great way to "chat" with each child about topics of interest; however, this can also be rather time consuming. You may find it necessary to respond to each child's journal only once a week to make the task more manageable.

With traditional journal writing, you may find that children tend to write about their daily events and don't really attempt to get very creative in their written expression. It is important to help the children find a direction in their journal writing. Some children will choose to write stories, others will share personal experiences, while others will write questions they hope you will answer. The most important thing is that each child finds a meaningful way to use his or her journal.

The Journal

Just about anything can be used for a journal. Students need to have opportunities to write on all kinds of paper. The following are some journal ideas.

- composition books—The pages can be completely lined or half lined and half blank for drawing pictures.
- spiral notebooks—These are great for daily writing. The students enjoy being able to look back and see their progress over the course of the school year.
- blank paper—Several sheets of blank paper can be stapled together to make a journal.
- lined paper
- blank books
- diaries
- binders filled with paper
- folders filled with paper
- monthly or seasonal shape books
- notepads

See pages 22 and 23 for journal pages to duplicate and bind for student use.

The Journal *(cont.)*

Scrapbook journals are a great way to add interest and variety to the journal writing experience.

These unique journals can be used with your children for collecting pictures of family members or pets. They can attach drawings or artwork to the pages. Encourage the use of writing to tell about the items included. Several pages might be used to tell a story to accompany a photo or a drawing. This kind of scrapbook is fun to read and share with others. Encourage your children to be creative with the items they include and allow them to share their journals with classmates for enjoyment and for inspiration.

Writing Memoir

Writing memoir is merely writing stories about one's life. Typically, children write in their journals about what happened yesterday or last weekend. Encourage your children to think back several years to write stories about their lives.

- What is your earliest memory?
- What is a special time you spent with your dad? your mom?
- Does your family have any special holiday traditions?
- What was the happiest day of your life?
- Think of a time when you were really afraid.
- What is your favorite memory of your grandmother? your grandfather?
- What is your favorite family memory?

Your children may want to make lists of stories they would like to tell. Writing your memoirs doesn't have to happen all at once. Just encourage the children to begin writing stories of their lives. Bit by bit the memoir comes together. Get your students started by writing in response to the questions on page 25.

Share some of the children's books below (written in first person) to inspire the writing of memoir.

- *When I Was Young in the Mountains* by Cynthia Rylant
- *The Relatives Came* by Cynthia Rylant
- *Owl Moon* by Jane Yolen
- *Little House in the Big Woods* by Laura Ingalls Wilder
- *Alexander, Who Used to Be Rich Last Sunday* by Judith Viorst
- *A Chair for My Mother* by Vera B. Williams
- *Stringbean's Trip to the Shining Sea* by Vera B. Williams
- *The Wreck of the Zephyr* by Chris Van Allsburg
- *I'll Fix Anthony* by Judith Viorst
- *Gila Monsters Meet You at the Airport* by Marjorie Weinman Sharmat

Teacher's Guide

My School Year Memory Book

Photographs are a great way to get students actively involved in the writing process. A digital camera is a great cost saver, but if you don't have access to one, let parents know that you need film for a special project. Many parents would be more than willing to donate several rolls of film to the class. Some might even be willing to pay for the developing costs. Throughout the school year, take pictures of the students as they are involved in different types of activities such as art projects, reading groups, seatwork, plays, etc. Then follow these steps to prepare each memory book:

1. Create a cover on cardstock and write the child's name on it. Use cardstock for the back cover also. (You can also duplicate page 26 and glue it to the cardstock for a cover.)

2. Take a picture of the student at the beginning of the year and paste it to the center of the cover.

3. Place 12–15 blank pages in the book and staple the book together. (You can also duplicate page 27 to include as the inside pages of the memory book.)

4. At the beginning of the school year, have each student write his or her name.

5. About every six weeks (or whenever you have several new rolls of film developed) place photographs in baskets and give each group a basket. Let the students pick out several pictures each that they are in.

6. On 2" x 7" (5 cm x 18 cm) strips of paper, have the students write sentences that tell about what was happening when the pictures were taken. (At the beginning of the school year, some students might need to dictate their sentences.)

7. Have the students bring the completed strips and their pictures to you. Check to make sure that the pictures are not already in their memory books. Review the sentences with the students. Then glue the pictures and the sentences into their memory books.

8. Toward the end of the school year, take several pictures of the whole class. These pictures can be glued to the inside of the back cover of each student's memory book.

At Open House, place the memory books on the students' desks. The students and their parents will be thrilled to see the school year through the students' eyes.

Student Page

Journal Page

Journal Page

Writing Memoir

1. What is your earliest memory?

_____

_____

_____

2. What is a special time you spent with your dad or your mom?

_____

_____

_____

3. Does your family have any special holiday traditions?

_____

_____

_____

4. What was the happiest day of your life?

_____

_____

_____

5. Think of a time when you were really afraid.

_____

_____

_____

6. What is your favorite memory of your grandmother or your grandfather?

_____

_____

_____

7. What is your favorite family memory?

_____

_____

Writing Memoir

Use this page to assist you in writing a story that happened in your life.

- What was the event?

  _____

- Who was there?

  _____

  _____

- How did this event make you feel?

  _____

- Where were you when this happened?

  _____

  _____

- How old were you? _____

- Why was this event important to remember?

  _____

  _____

- Write a story telling about this memory.

  _____

  _____

  _____

  _____

  _____

  _____

- Draw a picture to go with your story.

_____'s

Memory Book

Year:

_____

Memory Book Page

This picture shows: _____

Here's what happened:

_____

_____

_____

_____

_____

_____

Phonemic Awareness Activities

Phonemic awareness refers to an individual's ability to attend to the sounds of spoken words. In order to begin to read and write, a child needs to understand that words are made up of individual sounds. It is important to remember that phonemic awareness activities should be fun and playful for the children.

Why Teach Phonemic Awareness?

Research suggests that experience with and instruction of phonemic awareness benefits children in their quest to become readers and writers. Phonemic awareness assists children in spelling and should be related to letters in order to assist them with transitioning from hearing sounds to reading words.

As described in the report of The National Reading Panel, there are several elements involved in phonemic awareness instruction. These include the following elements:

Phoneme Isolation—recognizing sounds in words

Example: The first sound in *dog* is /d/.

Phoneme Identity—recognizing words that have similar sounds

Example: The words *cat*, *car*, and *cave* all begin with /c/.

Phoneme Categorization—recognizing words that sound the same and words that sound different

Example: The words *bun*, *run*, and *fun* have similar sounds. The word *bat* does not sound the same.

Phoneme Blending—combining spoken phonemes into words

Example: The sounds /t//u//g/ make the word *tug*.

Phoneme Segmentation—breaking words into their separate phonemes

Example: There are four sounds in the word *truck* (/t//r//u//k/).

Phoneme Deletion—identifying a new word when a phoneme is removed from another word

Example: If you take away the /s/ in *start*, you have the word *tart*.

Phoneme Addition—identifying a new word when a phoneme is added to another word

Example: If you add /s/ to the beginning of *port*, you have the word *sport*.

Phoneme Substitution—changing a phoneme in a word to make a new word

Example: If you change the /r/ in *car* to /t/, you have the word *cat*.

When conducting phonemic awareness activities, focus only on one or two of these elements at a time. Keep in mind, also, that you may teach phonemic awareness in a variety of formats—whole group, small group, or individual instruction. You will need to determine which format best suits the needs of your students.

Phonemic Awareness Activities *(cont.)*

Teacher's Guide

What's Your Name?

1. Gather your students together for a name game.

2. Ask each child to tell the sound that is heard at the beginning of his or her name. *Jennifer* begins with the sound /j/.

3. After students identify the sounds at the beginning of their names, instruct them to organize themselves into groups based on the sounds at the beginning of their names. For example, all of the students with /m/ at the beginning should stand together.

4. Be sure to discuss the fact that sometimes different letters make the same sound. For example, Kylie and Carrie begin with different letters, but make the same sound.

What Do You Hear?

1. Ask students to listen for sounds they hear at the ends of words.

2. Begin by saying a single word, such as *dog*. Ask the students, "What sound do you hear at the end of *dog*?"

3. Emphasize the sound as you say it for students who need assistance.

4. Continue this activity by saying two or three words with the same ending sound, such as *mat, bat, hit*. "What sound do you hear at the end of these words?" See below for groups of words to use for practice.

Words ending in /b/	Words ending in /r/
• grab • sob • bib	• car • tear • roar
Words ending in /m/	**Words ending in /s/**
• hum • mom • game	• kiss • house • bass
Words ending in /l/	**Words ending in /d/**
• doll • school • drill	• had • kid • said

Picture Sounds

This activity assists your students with identification of sounds in words.

Materials

- picture cards (pages 30–33)
- crayons and markers (optional)
- scissors

1. Duplicate the cards below and on pages 31–33. Color and laminate the cards, if desired, and cut them apart.

2. Show the students how to use the cards. A student selects a card from the stack and says the name of the picture.

3. Ask the student questions, such as the following:
   - What sound do you hear at the beginning of the word?
   - What sound do you hear at the end of the word?
   - Can you think of another word that begins with the same sound?
   - Can you think of another word that ends with the same sound?

Continue in this manner, giving all students the opportunity to participate. Place the cards in a learning center and encourage the students to continue practice on their own or with partners.

Picture Cards

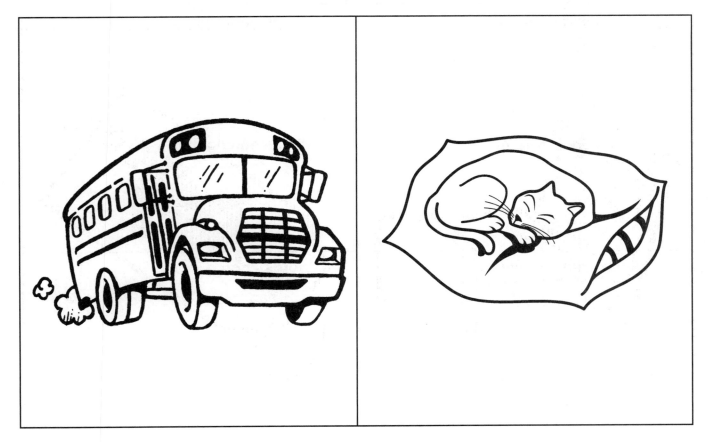

Picture Cards

Picture Cards

Picture Cards

Phonemic Awareness Activities *(cont.)*

Sound Detectives

1. Gather students together. Explain that you will say three words. Their job is to determine which sound is the same in each word.

2. Begin by saying three words with the same beginning sound, such as *ball*, *baby*, and *bit*. After students identify that each word has the /b/ sound, ask them which word contains that sound more than once (*baby*).

3. Try this with several groups of words with the same beginning sound.

4. Make the activity more challenging by saying groups of words with the same ending sound, middle sound, or a combination of these. See below for groups of words.

Same Beginning Sound	Same Middle Sound
dog, duck, dive	bun, tough, truck
my, mix, motor	cat, tag, man
sale, sit, sample	pin, mix, did
Same Ending Sound	**Combination**
hit, get, barrette	sip, pig, lamp
high, sky, lie	try, ice, like
make, soak, kick	simple, mill, trim

Which Word Doesn't Belong?

1. For this activity, your students will be asked to identify the word in a set of three that does not sound the same as the others.

2. Say the words *bun*, *fun*, and *cake*. Ask the students to identify which word doesn't belong.

3. Ask the students to explain why the word is different. Try this activity with rhyming words as well as with words that have same and different beginning and ending sounds.

4. To make the activity more challenging, have your students listen for similar and different blends. See below for sample word groups.

Rhyming/Not Rhyming	Beginning Sound	Blends
try, fly, wake	candle, light, came	snake, snail, slide
coat, float, trick	funny, many, miner	treat, trick, tail
make, sit, mitt	house, hat, shower	glow, green, gram
stable, cable, ready	kitchen, kite, fish	brow, brick, blow

Phonemic Awareness Activities *(cont.)*

Sound Riddles

Phoneme blending is the ability to combine spoken phonemes into words.

1. Play a sound blending game with your students.

2. Think of a word and say the separate sounds that make up the word, such as /t/ /r/ /u/ /k/.

3. The students listen to the sounds and combine them to make the word *truck*.

4. Begin by using shorter words and increase the difficulty with longer words. (See the lists below.)

5. Allow the students to think of their own words to share with the class in the same manner.

One-Syllable Words			Two-Syllable Words		
track	→	/t/ /r/ /a/ /k/	carpet	→	/c/ /a/ /r/ /p/ /e/ /t/
dog	→	/d/ /o/ /g/	table	→	/t/ /a/ /b/ /l/
cup	→	/c/ /u/ /p/	desert	→	/d/ /e/ /s/ /r/ /t/
pill	→	/p/ /i/ /l/	closet	→	/c/ /l/ /o/ /s/ /e/ /t/
brush	→	/b/ /r/ /u/ /sh/	baseball	→	/b/ /a/ /s/ /b/ /a/ /l/

Tracking Sounds

Using this activity will help your students to identify the number of sounds in a word.

Materials

- copy of page 36 (laminated) for each student
- wipe-off markers

1. This activity gives your students the chance to determine the number of individual phonemes or sounds in words.

2. Prepare for the activity by duplicating and laminating the chart on page 36 for each student. Provide each child with a wipe-off marker.

3. To play, the teacher says a word and has each child think of the number of individual sounds he or she can hear in the word.

4. The child makes an **X** for each sound heard. For example, the child would mark **XXXX** for the word glass (/g/ /l/ /a/ /s/).

5. After completing this for each word, show the children the actual spelling of the word and discuss the fact that not all letters in a word are represented by separate sounds.

6. To use this as a learning center activity, make a tape recording of your voice slowly pronouncing a series of words.

7. Students listen to the words on the tape recording and mark on the chart the number of sounds they hear.

Tracking Sounds

Say or listen to a word. Draw an **X** to represent each sound you hear in the word.

1.					
2.					
3.					
4.					
5.					
6.					

Phonemic Awareness Activities *(cont.)*

What's Left?

This activity encourages your students to be sound detectives.

1. Say a word and then ask the children to determine what the word would change to if a sound is removed. For example, "What word is left if we remove the /s/ from smile?" (mile)

2. Continue in this manner. A list of these riddles is provided below.

   * What word is left if we remove the /t/ in trust?   (*rust*)
   * What word is left if we remove the /c/ in cable.   (*able*)
   * What word is left if we remove the /t/ in plant?   (*plan*)
   * What word is left if we remove the /n/ in snake?   (*sake*)
   * What word is left if we remove the /d/ in board?   (*boar*)
   * What word is left if we remove the /c/ in cat?   (*at*)
   * What word is left if we remove the /n/ in brown?   (*brow*)
   * What word is left if we remove the /p/ in plate?   (*late*)
   * What word is left if we remove the /l/ in slick?   (*sick*)

Making New Words

Your children will determine the creation of new words with this activity.

1. To play, say a word. Then ask how the word would change if a particular sound were added. For example, "Listen to the word *flee*. What word do we have if we add /t/ at the end?" (*fleet*)

2. Continue in this manner with the words listed below. Allow the children to create some of their own phonemic additions.

   * ben /ch/   * clam /p/   * /a/ cross
   * wind /y/   * gas /p/   * /s/ car
   * plan /t/   * fir /st/   * /t/rip

Presto Change-o!

Similar to the activity above, the children determine how a word changes when one sound is replaced with another.

1. To play, say a word. Then ask how the word would change if a particular sound were substituted for another. For example, "Listen to the word *trip*. What word would we have if we changed the /p/ to /m/?" (*trim*)

2. Continue in this manner with the words listed below. Allow the children to create some of their own phonemic substitutions.

   * dog/log   * leather/weather
   * pit/pin   * dinner/winner
   * cat/can   * paper/pager
   * tale/tame

Group Writing Experiences

Writing as a group on a regular basis provides your students with a model of the skills and thought processes involved in quality writing.

Daily Tasks

Begin each day with a discussion of the day's daily tasks, including special classes and regular subject areas. Rather than listing these tasks for the students, ask them to dictate these tasks as you write them on a chart (see page 41 for a template to enlarge). This daily routine will provide a model for good writing while helping them organize for the day.

Story Dictation

A routine of story dictation is extremely beneficial to your students. It allows them to think about story structure, develop characters and settings, and play off the ideas of classmates.

1. To prepare for dictation, gather the students and discuss a possible story topic or main character.

2. Then ask the children to determine some of the events that could happen in the story. Determine main events of the beginning, middle, and ending.

3. When the students are ready to begin the story, have them take turns saying a sentence of the story, after which you write it on chart paper.

4. Save group stories and encourage students to read through them from time to time.

Weekly News

1. Report to parents the main events of the week with a weekly news bulletin.

2. Unlike a newsletter that you write to inform parents of the week's activities, this newsletter highlights an event or activity that the children want to share for each day of the week. For example, "On Monday we got a new hamster. We named her Katie."

3. Have the students determine and dictate an event for each day of the week.

4. Then duplicate the newsletter and send it home to parents on Friday. (See page 42 for Weekly News template.)

5. Have students refer to page 240 of the Writer's Notebook for news article templates.

Group Stories

By participating in this fun activity, your students will practice implementing what they know about story structure.

1. Gather the students together in a circle and explain that they will be creating a group story.

2. Remind them that stories have specific characters, settings, and events.

3. Remind them also that there are events that happen at the beginning, middle, and end of the story and that these events are interrelated.

Group Writing Experiences *(cont.)*

Group Stories *(cont.)*

4. Tell the students that they must listen carefully to the information contributed by other classmates so they can create a story that is clear and organized.

5. Begin the story by stating the setting and main character. (You could also designate a student to begin the story.)

6. Another student takes over the story and adds an event or description.

7. Continue in this manner until all students have had the chance to contribute to the story.

8. Take time to review the completed story, identifying the main characters, setting, and beginning, middle, and ending events.

9. To make this activity even more interesting, fill a bag with different small objects, such as a leaf, a ball, a key, a handkerchief, etc.

10. As students are telling their portions of the story, periodically hand the bag to a student and ask him or her to reach in and take out an object. The object selected must then be included in the story in some way.

Writing a Summary

Writing a story summary in a group writing setting is a great way to teach summarizing.

1. Explain that sometimes it is necessary to tell about a story using only a few sentences. This is called summarizing. For example, if you went on a vacation to Disneyland, there would be a lot of things to talk about.

2. If you were to tell someone about your trip, you might find it necessary to tell about the vacation by summarizing the important highlights of the trip.

3. Write the following sentences on the chalkboard and review them with the students.

- My family went to Disneyland.
- We went to the haunted house.
- We rode on the teacups.
- We snacked on chocolate covered bananas.
- We also ate a big lunch in Tomorrowland.
- At night we saw the light parade.
- I was so tired that I fell asleep on the drive home.

Writing a Summary *(cont.)*

4. Next, ask the students to think about a way to tell about this trip using only two or three sentences. See below for a suggestion.

> My family went to Disneyland. We went on lots of rides and ate good food.

5. Have the students dictate story summaries to you as you write them on the chalkboard.

Paraphrasing

Practice with paraphrasing will help your students to better summarize stories.

1. Review with the students the meaning of summarizing. Remind them that when a story is summarized, it is retold using just a few sentences. Summarizing involves telling the main idea of the story and a few important details. For example, if we summarize the story *Cinderella*, we might say this:

> Cinderella had a mean family. They made her do all of the work. Then she went to a party and met a prince. They fell in love, and she didn't have to live with her family anymore.

2. Draw students' attention to the fact that only four sentences were used to retell the story.

3. Then explain to students that when we retell a story, we don't use the exact words of the author. We use our own words. This is called paraphrasing.

4. Practice paraphrasing as a group by reading aloud a story and then allowing students to offer their paraphrased summaries as you write them on chart paper. (If students use exact words from the story, assist them in changing the words.)

5. For additional practice, have the students complete page 44.

Daily Tasks Chart

Time	Subject/Activity

Weekly News Template

Monday

_____

_____

_____

_____

Tuesday

_____

_____

_____

_____

Wednesday

_____

_____

_____

_____

Thursday

_____

_____

_____

_____

Friday

_____

_____

_____

_____

Summary Guide

Use this page to assist with writing a summary of a book or movie.

1. Who were the main characters?

   _____

   _____

2. How did the story begin?

   _____

   _____

3. Where did the story take place?

   _____

   _____

4. What problem happened in the story?

   _____

   _____

5. How did the story end?

   _____

   _____

6. What was your favorite part?

   _____

   _____

   Write a summary of the story using five sentences or fewer.

   _____

   _____

   _____

   _____

   _____

Paraphrasing Practice

Read the information and rewrite it using your own words.
(*Teacher Note*: Assist students with reading the information as needed.)

> **Example:** A tornado is a column of rotating air inside a cloud that touches the earth's surface.
>
> **Paraphrase:** A tornado is air that spins and touches the ground.

1. Rain forests are usually located in regions where there is a high annual rainfall.

   Paraphrase: _____

   _____

2. A blizzard is an extreme weather event that is characterized by strong winds, low temperatures, and large quantities of snow.

   Paraphrase: _____

   _____

3. Dairy products are foods made from milk, such as cheese and ice cream.

   Paraphrase: _____

   _____

4. The cheetah is a long-legged cat that is facing extinction.

   Paraphrase: _____

   _____

Sentence Writing

Use the activities in this section to assist your children in writing complete sentences with correct punctuation and capitalization.

Complete Sentences

This activity will help your students to create simple sentences.

1. Gather your students together and display the following sentences on chart paper:
   - Kelly is a good.
   - Kelly is a good artist.

2. Ask the students to read the sentences and then discuss them. Is there something wrong with one of the sentences?

3. Lead them to identify that the first sentence is incomplete. It tells us that Kelly is good at something, but it doesn't tell us what.

4. Continue discussion with the following sentences:
   - The dog.
   - The dog ran.
   - The can is full of.
   - The can is full of beans.

5. Draw students' attention to the fact that a complete sentence has a subject and an action and represents a complete thought.

6. Have students practice making their own simple sentences using pages 46-48.

Writing Questions and Statements

Help your students determine the difference between questions and statements with this short lesson.

1. Write the following sentences on the chalkboard, omitting the punctuation.
   - Have you been there before
   - This is my house
   - Are you coming over
   - Tell me how to do this

2. Explain to your students that sentences always end with a punctuation mark.

3. We need to determine whether each sentence is telling something or asking something.

4. *Telling* sentences end with periods, and *asking* sentences end with question marks.

5. Review each of the sentences above and determine the punctuation needed.

6. Have students practice this skill using pages 49 and 50.

Expanding Sentences

For practice in adding details to both statements and questions, have students use the exercises on pages 51–53.

Complete Sentences

car

gray

little

fast

broken

white

black

Create your own sentences using the words above.

1. The car is _____

2. The car _____

3. The _____

4. _____

Complete Sentences

Create your own sentences using the words above.

1. The pizza is _____

2. The pizza _____

3. The _____

4. _____

Complete Sentences

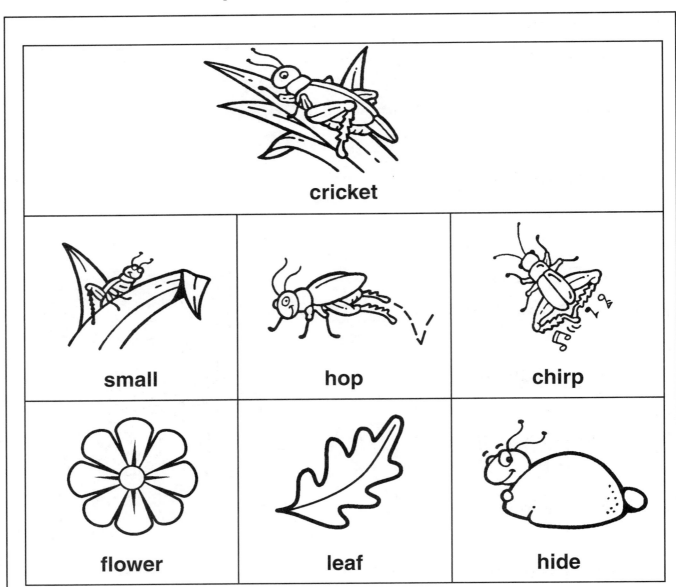

cricket

small

hop

chirp

flower

leaf

hide

Create your own sentences using the words above.

1. The cricket is _____

2. The cricket _____

3. The _____

4. _____

Questions and Statements

Write the correct punctuation mark at the end of each sentence.

1. The butterfly is beautiful _____

2. Have you seen a butterfly before _____

3. You're my best friend _____

4. That's a nice shirt _____

5. How old are you _____

6. This is my dog _____

7. What time is it _____

8. Be careful not to fall down _____

9. Let's go to the library _____

10. Can you help me lift the box _____

Questions and Statements

Change each statement into a question. Write the new sentence on the line. Don't forget to use correct punctuation.

1. It's a nice spring day.

   _____

   _____

2. I think I saw your brother in the lunch room.

   _____

   _____

3. It's time to plant the garden.

   _____

   _____

4. I just love playing soccer.

   _____

   _____

5. That's my favorite book.

   _____

   _____

6. Take your time on the spelling test.

   _____

   _____

7. That man is my father.

   _____

   _____

8. I had fun at the baseball game.

   _____

   _____

Sentence Expanding

Write a word in each blank below to expand the sentences. If you need help, use the words in the Word Box.

1. The _____ cat is soft.

2. That _____ car is fast.

3. It's a lovely _____ day.

4. Trisha is a _____, _____ girl.

5. I can smell the _____ pizza.

6. The _____ boy fell down.

7. I saw the _____, _____ elephant.

8. Did you see the _____ giraffe?

Word Box

fresh	spring	big	little
black	nice	gray	clumsy
tall	young		

Expanding Sentences

Read each sentence below. Then rewrite the sentence adding details to make the sentence more interesting.

1. The teacher is nice.

   _____

   _____

2. There is a big tree in the yard.

   _____

   _____

3. I'll be working in the library.

   _____

   _____

4. Listen to the bird sing.

   _____

   _____

5. She plays the guitar.

   _____

   _____

6. Look at the candles.

   _____

   _____

7. I like those flowers.

   _____

   _____

8. Let's go to the park.

   _____

   _____

Sentence Pyramid

Read the sentence pyramid below. Notice how the sentence is changed by adding one new word or so each time.

I saw a bee.

I saw a yellow bee.

I saw a yellow bee flying.

I saw a yellow bee flying quickly.

I saw a yellow bee flying quickly in the air.

I saw a yellow bee flying quickly in the air yesterday.

Write a sentence pyramid of your own.

I saw a _____.

I saw a _____ _____.

I saw a _____ _____ _____.

I saw a _____ _____ _____ _____.

I saw a _____ _____ _____ _____ _____.

I saw a _____ _____ _____ _____ _____ _____.

Story Writing

Using a Story Map

A story map can be used to display the sequence of events in a story. When teaching your students how to use a story map, enlist their help (as a group) to map the events of a story read to the class.

1. Post a large sheet of bulletin-board paper or chart paper for all to see.

2. Then begin by drawing a circle or a square. The first event of the story is written inside the shape. (Allow the students to offer their ideas for the events to be written on the map.)

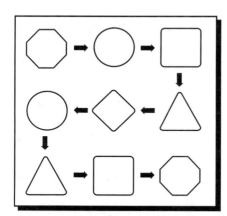

3. Draw an arrow following the shape and then draw another shape and write the next story event inside it.

4. Continue in this manner until the map is complete. (See the illustration for an example.)

5. You can also provide a flow chart (page 73) for students to create their own story maps.

6. Have students refer to the story structure sheet on page 252 of the Writer's Notebook.

Picture Stories

In this activity, students use pictures to tell a story.

1. Gather students together for a story. Display a wordless picture book, such as *George Shrinks* by William Joyce (see page 55 for other book titles) and tell them that the book uses pictures rather than words to tell the story.

2. Show the students the pages of the story and discuss the details shown in the pictures.

3. After completing the story, ask students to tell the events that happened at the beginning, middle, and end. Also, ask them about the problem and solution in the story.

4. Draw their attention to the fact that these elements of the story were conveyed through pictures only.

5. Then instruct students to create their own picture stories, drawing each event of the story on a different sheet of paper.

6. You can assemble their pictures into wordless books or have them use their pictures as inspiration for writing stories.

Wordless (or almost wordless) Books

❏ *Anno's Counting Book* by Anno Mitsumasa

❏ *Changes, Changes* by Pat Hutchins

❏ *Clementina's Cactus* by Ezra Jack Keats

❏ *Dinosaur!* by Peter Sís

❏ *Do You Want to Be My Friend?* by Tomie DePaola

❏ *Follow Carl!* by Alexandra Day

❏ *Four Hungry Kittens* by Emily Arnold McCully

❏ *Free Fall* by David Wiesner

❏ *Good Dog, Carl* by Alexandra Day

❏ *Home* by Jeannie Baker

❏ *Mysteries of Harris Burdick* by Chris Van Allsburg

❏ *An Ocean World* by Peter Sis

❏ *One Frog Too Many* by Mercer Mayer

❏ *Pancakes for Breakfast* by Tomie dePaola

❏ *Peter Spier's Rain* by Peter Spier

❏ *Rosie's Walk* by Pat Hutchins

❏ *Sector 7* by David Wiesner

❏ *The Snowman* by Raymond Briggs

❏ *Tabby: A Story in Pictures* by Aliki

❏ *Tuesday* by David Wiesner

❏ *Window* by Jeannie Baker

Writing Traits: Ideas and Content

Ideas and Content Overview

The ideas and content trait helps students gather and organize their ideas. This trait is particularly appropriate and necessary for young writers as it allows them to think about and plan their writing. This trait also helps children to identify the need for details and helps them to notice particular formats that authors use in their books. You will notice that practice with this trait will bring about a higher level of writing from your children. (Duplicate the Ideas poster on page 59 to display in your classroom.)

Brainstorming

It is important to allow children to think about and brainstorm writing topics before they begin writing. Simply providing children with a story title and telling them to begin writing can be frustrating for most children.

1. Gather the children together and begin a simple discussion. What kinds of things could we write about today? Do you have a particular kind of character on your mind? Is there an event you would like to write about?

2. Write their ideas on chart paper and display the ideas for several days. Remind the students to review the list before writing in order to gain new ideas.

3. Provide a copy of page 60 for each student to keep in a writing notebook. As the student thinks of ideas for writing, have him or her write the idea on the page for later use.

Group Brainstorming

Brainstorming in small groups is extremely helpful to young children.

1. After the students have had the opportunity to think about writing topics, group the students in twos or threes.

2. Have the students share their story ideas.

3. Encourage group members to comment on these ideas, ask questions, and add ideas of their own. For example, if a student says, "I think I'm going to write a story about a horse," another student might ask, "Will it be a talking horse?" or "What will the horse be named?" Another student might interject, "Oh, it could be a race horse!"

4. Encourage the children to listen to the group members' comments and ideas, even if they have different directions for their stories.

5. This group interaction not only helps to provide the writer with new ideas but also helps the student to better define his or her original ideas for writing the story.

Writing Traits: Ideas and Content *(cont.)*

Idea Web

Idea webs and character webs are great tools for assisting children in developing stories. The idea web on page 61 can be used to help children organize initial thoughts about a story.

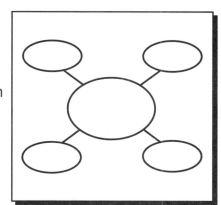

1. Begin by doing a group activity using an idea web.

2. Draw the web on chart paper and select a topic for a story.

3. Write the topic in the center circle.

4. Then ask the students to suggest events that might happen in the story.

5. Write these ideas in the surrounding circles.

6. Explain to the children that ideas related to each of the events can be written surrounding the individual circles.

Character Web

The character web on page 62 can be used to assist children in the development of important characters for their stories.

1. Before using the web to develop their own characters, have children complete the web with a character from a familiar story. The student will identify basic information about the character as well as more critical information, such as personality traits, actions, and likes/dislikes.

2. When the students are comfortable with identifying these characteristics of story characters, encourage them to use the character web to develop characters for their own story writing.

Patterned Writing

Drawing students' attention to patterns that authors use in writing can give children their own ideas for writing.

1. For example, the story *Alexander and the Terrible, Horrible, No Good, Very Bad Day* by Judith Viorst has a very specific pattern. Alexander tells about several bad things that happened to him, and then he says, "It was a terrible, horrible, no good, very bad day."

2. Read the story aloud to the children and ask them to identify this pattern.

3. Suggest to the students that they, too, could write stories about bad days or good days in the same pattern that Judith Viorst uses.

Fractured Fairy Tales

Children enjoy fractured fairy tales and often enjoy comparing these outrageous fairy tale versions to the originals.

1. Read several fractured fairy tales (see suggested books below) to your students and then ask them to think about a tale they could rewrite in a humorous way.

2. Provide each student with a copy of page 63 for planning a fractured tale.

Suggested Books:

- *The True Story of the Three Little Pigs* by Jon Scieszka
- *Sleeping Ugly* by Jane Yolen
- *The Talking Eggs: a Folktale from the American South* by Robert San Souci
- *The Principal's New Clothes* by Stephanie Calmenson

Wordless Books

Wordless (or almost wordless) books can serve as excellent forms of writing information. As children browse through the illustrations that tell the story without words, they will likely want to write the story using their own interpretation of the illustrations. Share the following books with your students.

Suggested Books:

- *Pancakes for Breakfast* by Tomie de Paola
- *Rosie's Walk* by Pat Hutchins
- *Free Fall* by David Weisner
- *George Shrinks* by William Joyce
- *Dinosaur* by Peter Sis

Ideas and Content

This trait refers to the content of the writing.

☑ clear messages

☑ use of detail

☑ presentation of information

Ideas for Writing

My Writing Ideas

_____

_____

_____

_____

_____

_____

Character Ideas

_____

_____

_____

_____

_____

_____

Story Ideas

_____

_____

_____

_____

_____

Setting Ideas

_____

_____

_____

_____

_____

Idea Web

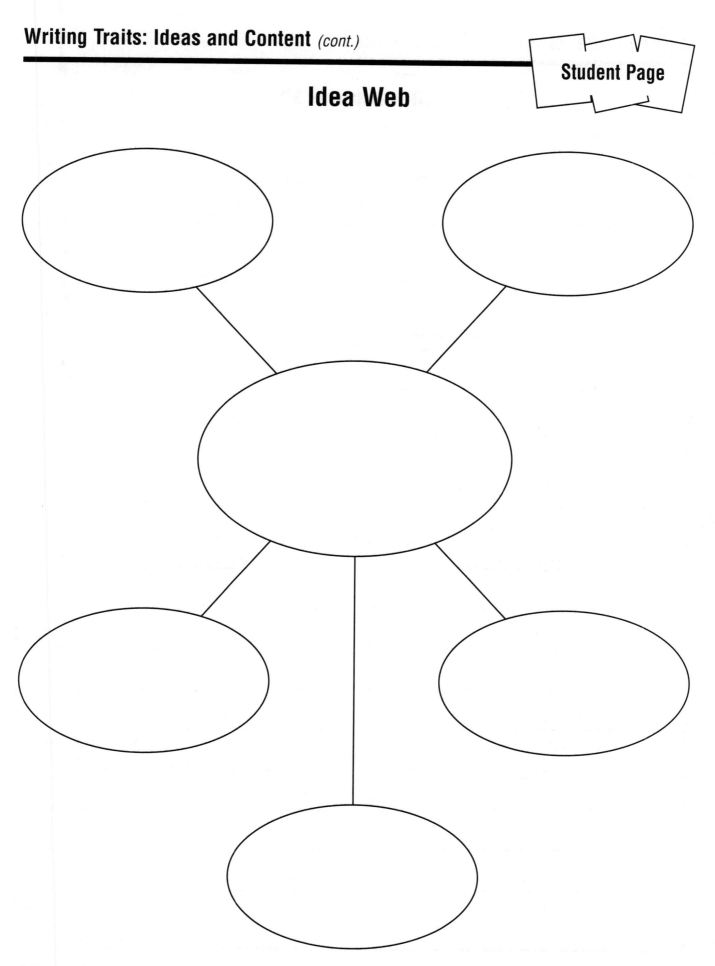

Character Web

Character Name

General Information **Personality** **Actions** **Feels Strongly About . . .**

Name | Trait 1 | Action 1 | 1

Age | Trait 2 | Action 2 | 2

Where she/he lives | Trait 3 | Action 3 | 3

Fractured Fairy Tale Planner

Name of Original Fairy Tale

_____

Write a summary of the original tale below.

_____

_____

_____

_____

_____

What is your plan for changing the fairy tale?

_____

_____

_____

_____

Write the name of each original character and the character that will be in the new version.

_____

• Original Characters

_____

_____

• New Characters

_____

_____

Write about your ideas for new story events. Use a story map to organize your ideas, if necessary.

_____

_____

_____

_____

Writing Traits: Organization

The trait of organization is an important element of the writing process. Writing with organization has a clear direction and logical sequence of events. (Use the Organization poster on page 67 to display in your classroom.)

Books for Teaching Organization

It is good to share books that exemplify a particular writing trait. Children enjoy books that reflect strong story organization, such as beginning/middle/end, event sequencing, actions/consequences, and story patterns. As you read these books aloud to your students, draw their attention to the structure or pattern of each story.

- *The Legend of the Bluebonnet* by Tomie dePaola (beginning/middle/end)
- *There's a Nightmare in My Closet* by Mercer Meyer (beginning/middle/end)
- *Two Bad Ants* by Chris Van Allsburg (actions/consequences)
- *Fables* by Arnold Lobel (actions/consequences)
- *A Chair for My Mother* by Vera B. Williams (sequence of events)
- *Cloudy with a Chance of Meatballs* by Judi Barrett (sequence of events)
- *Alexander and the Terrible, Horrible, No Good, Very Bad Day* by Judith Viorst (story pattern)
- *It Could Always Be Worse* by Margot Zemach (story pattern)

Sequencing

Explain to your students that the sequence of events in a story is very important. If events are not presented in a logical order, the story can be difficult to understand.

1. Begin by reading a story with a strong sequence of events, such as *Where the Wild Things Are* by Maurice Sendak.

2. Ask the students to think of the major events in the story (see below) and list them on sentence strips.

- Max makes mischief.
- Max is sent to his room.
- He travels by boat to where the wild things are.
- He rules over the wild things.
- Max and the wild things have a wild rumpus.
- Max leaves the wild things and travels home.
- He returns to find his supper waiting for him.

Writing Traits: Organization *(cont.)*

Sequencing *(cont.)*

3. Then display the sentence strips in a pocket chart (or taped to a chalkboard or easel) with a few of the events out of order.

4. Read the events and ask the students to tell why the new order upsets the sequence of the story. Does it make sense this way?

5. Draw their attention to the fact that when writing a story with previously brainstormed ideas, it is important to present each of the ideas or event in a sequence that makes sense.

6. Provide copies of the event sequencing sheet on page 68 for assistance in sequencing events for their own stories.

Beginning, Middle, and End

Learning basic story organization involves the ability to write a clear beginning, middle, and ending. Once again, this can be easily exhibited by sharing a story that clearly displays these elements, such as *Gregory, the Terrible Eater* by Mitchell Sharmat.

1. Before reading the story, divide a sheet of chart paper into three sections and label each—Beginning, Middle, End.

2. Explain to the children that as they listen to the story, they should try to identify the general event that represents each part of the story.

   Beginning—Gregory didn't want to eat the food his parents ate. Instead, he wanted to eat foods like fruits, vegetables, and fish.

   Middle—Gregory's parents are worried about him and they take him to the doctor to find out what's wrong.

   End—Gregory learns to eat a balanced diet.

3. Explain to the children that it is likely that the author had these ideas in mind when he began to write the story. As he wrote the story he added more details and description to make the story more enjoyable.

4. Provide students with copies of page 69 for beginning writers or page 70 for more advanced writing. These pages help students plan the beginning, middle, and ending events of their original stories.

Event Planning

Sometimes it's difficult for children (adults, too) to get started on a story because they can't think of the events they want to take place.

1. To assist your students with this, gather them together in a group and, as a group, think of a topic and main character.

Event Planning *(cont.)*

2. After thinking of a topic and main character, start brainstorming.
   - What could be the problem the character faces?
   - What could the character do to try to solve this problem?
   - Should there be any additional characters who help the main character?
   - What should they do together?
   - How would you like the main character's problem to be solved?

3. Then, on a sheet of chart paper, create the Event Planning Chart on page 71.

4. Review the chart and record the answers based on the group's ideas in the brainstorming session.

5. Explain to the children that this kind of chart can be used to develop ideas for the events of a story and can assist when writing the story.

6. Provide student copies of page 71 for beginning writers or page 72 for more advanced writers.

Using a Story Map

The story map on page 73 is a tool to be used for planning the order of events in a story.

1. Use this tool as a follow-up organizer after the completion of the idea web.

2. You will notice that the sections of the story map are connected by arrows, which indicate the order of the events.

3. Instruct students to write story events in the sections to indicate the order of events.

4. After the completion of the story map, the child is ready to begin writing.

Writing an Interesting Lead Sentence

Part of organizing a story (for more advanced writers) is creating a lead sentence that captures the reader's attention.

1. Explain to the students that they can think of an interesting lead sentence as they begin writing a story, or they can add it later on.

2. Explain to students that there are many stories that people can read, but certain ones appeal to us more than others.

3. The first sentence of a story can make a big difference in a reader's choice to read or not read a particular story.

4. Distribute copies of page 74 and have students compare lead sentences, identifying the ones that are most interesting.

5. Then encourage them to think of ways to "spice up" their beginning sentences.

Organization

This refers to the structure of the writing.

- ☑ logical sequence of events

- ☑ organizing story events

- ☑ strong connections between parts of the story

- ☑ clear beginning, middle, and end

Event Sequencing

Read a story you wrote. Write each event in the order it happens in your story.

1. _____

2. _____

3. _____

4. _____

5. _____

6. _____

7. _____

8. _____

9. _____

10. _____

❑ Read numbers 1, 2, and 3. Does it make sense for these events to follow each other? _____

❑ Read numbers 3, 4, and 5. Does it make sense for these events to follow each other? _____

❑ Read numbers 5, 6, and 7. Does it make sense for these events to follow each other? _____

❑ Are the end events in the correct order?

❑ What information is missing that might help the reader to understand the story better? _____

❑ Where should that information be added? (After which event?)

❑ Rewrite the story on another sheet of paper.

Beginning, Middle, End

Think about the story you want to write.

What is the name of the main character?

_____

Draw a picture of this character.

What will your character do first?

_____
_____
_____

What will the character do next?

_____
_____
_____

What will the character do at the end of the story?

_____
_____
_____

Draw a picture of something that happens in the story.

Beginning, Middle, End (advanced)

Think about the story you want to write.

Who is the main character?

_____

Describe this character. How will your story begin?

_____

_____

_____

_____

What kind of problem will the character have?

_____

_____

_____

_____

What things will happen in the middle of the story?

_____

_____

_____

_____

How will the problem be solved?

_____

_____

_____

_____

What things will happen at the end of the story?

_____

_____

_____

Now you're ready to write! Be sure to add lots of details to your story.

Event Planning Chart

Draw a picture of the first thing that happens in the story.

Draw a picture of what happens next.

Draw a picture of what the character will do next.

Draw a picture showing something that happens at the end.

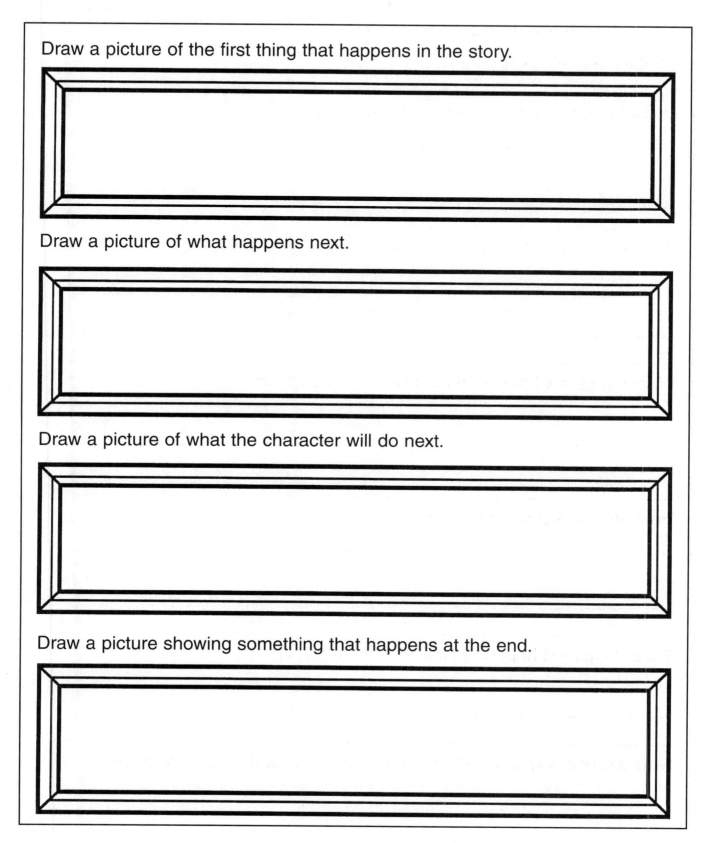

Event Planning Chart (advanced)

Who is the main character in the story? _____

What is the character's name? _____

What is his/her personality like? _____

_____

_____

_____

What could be the problem the character faces?

_____

_____

_____

What could the character do to try to solve this problem?

_____

_____

_____

Does the main character have any friends who will be in the story? Who are the friends? _____

_____

_____

What should the friends do together?

_____

_____

_____

How will the main character's problem be solved?

_____

_____

_____

_____

Use the information above to help you as you write your story.

Story Map

(This will look like a flow chart with squares connected by arrows showing the sequence of events.)

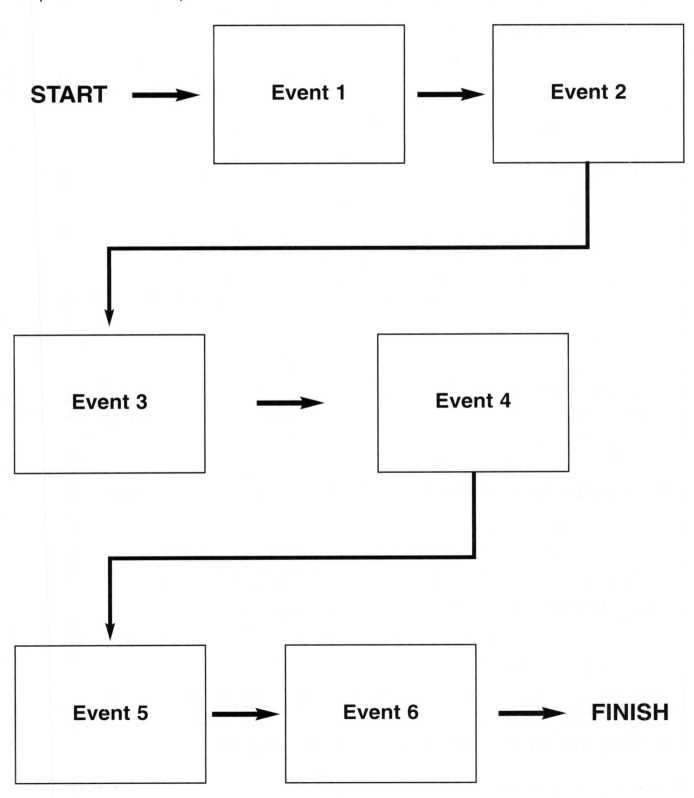

Interesting or Not?

Read each pair of lead sentences. Put an X in the box in front of the most interesting sentence. Then write a sentence telling why you liked that sentence the best.

1. ☐ It was a beautiful day, and Kelly was on her way to school.

2. ☐ It all happened on a beautiful day as Kelly walked to school.

_____

_____

3. ☐ Once upon a time a boy found a puppy.

4. ☐ You will never believe what happened on the day Freddy got a puppy.

_____

_____

5. ☐ Have you ever wondered what would happen if the sun disappeared for a day?

6. ☐ One day I woke up in the morning and it was dark outside.

_____

_____

7. ☐ It was the most exciting day of the year.

8. ☐ Mike went to the fair.

_____

_____

Writing Traits: Voice

The trait of voice focuses on the way an author expresses himself or herself. It can also refer to the voice or expression given to a particular character in a story. This can be a difficult trait to teach young children, so it is important to begin by having them identify voice in the stories they listen to or read. (Use the Voice poster on page 76 to display in your classroom.)

Identifying a Character's Voice

1. Draw students' attention to voice by reading aloud a story where the character expresses his or her mood through dialog. For example, in *Where the Wild Things Are* by Maurice Sendak, Max uses an angry and bossy voice. In *Charlotte's Web* by E.B. White, Charlotte often speaks to Wilbur in a very calm voice.
2. Emphasize the mood expressed as you read the story aloud.

Voices on Display

Allow the children to dramatize dialog, using voices that express particular moods.

1. Write the following sentence on the chalkboard: "Oh, look, it's raining outside."
2. Ask a student to say the sentence aloud as if he or she was happy about the rain.
3. Ask another student to repeat the same sentence as if he or she didn't want it to rain.
4. You might even give students scenarios to think about as they determine the voices to use.

Scenario #1

Imagine that you are going to a carnival after school. You have waited a whole year for the carnival to come to town. Today is the only day your family is able to go. When school is out, you open the door to the outside and it's raining. You know that the carnival will be canceled because of the weather.

Scenario #2

It is the middle of summer and it's hot outside. It hasn't rained for more than a month. The grass is beginning to turn brown and plants are dying. You know that many wild animals need water to drink and they also need plants to eat. You are very worried for them. You look outside and see that it is starting to rain.

5. Have students complete page 77 for more practice.

Voice and Punctuation

1. Explain to your children that voice can be expressed in writing by using punctuation marks.
2. Write the following sentences on the chalkboard:
   • That's a cute dog.   • That's a cute dog!
3. Ask students to pay attention to the punctuation marks. How do these marks change the way the sentences should be read?
4. Have the students practice reading the sentences with different expressions and voices.
5. Then have them write their own identical sentences using periods and exclamation marks.
6. Provide your students with more practice by completing page 78.

Voice

This trait refers to the voice of the writer coming through in the writing. It gives the story feeling and individuality.

☑ words that show a character's voice

☑ punctuation that conveys voice

Character Voice

Read each scenario below. Write a sentence or two expressing the voice you would use. The first one has been done for you.

1. You are going to a carnival after school if the weather is nice. You have waited a long time to go. Today is the only day your family is able to go. You look outside and it's raining. You say:

   "Oh, no! It's raining. Now we won't be able to go!"

   _____

2. You are having trouble with your homework. Your friend comes over to help you. Now it's easy to do. What do you say to your friend?

   _____

   _____

3. Your friend has a new baby brother. He is so small and cute. What would you say to the baby?

   _____

   _____

4. You are walking to school with your friend. Your friend bends down to tie his shoe. You see a car speeding around the corner. It is very close. What do you say to your friend?

   _____

   _____

5. It's the last day of school. You are going on vacation tomorrow. What do you say when the bell rings to go home?

   _____

   _____

6. It's almost time for lunch and you are really hungry. You smell food cooking in the lunchroom. It's pizza. What do you say?

   _____

   _____

What's the Mood?

Read each sentence. Circle the mood word expressed. Then rewrite the sentence in a different way to express another voice. The first one has been done for you.

1. Oh, no. That's a really scary ride.　**happy**　(**afraid**)　**mad**

　　Yea! We're going on a scary ride!
　　_____

2. Don't cut in line. It's my turn!　**happy**　**afraid**　**mad**

　　_____

　　_____

3. I don't want my friend to move away.　**happy**　**sad**　**afraid**

　　_____

　　_____

4. I can't wait to go to school! We're going on a field trip.
　　sad　**mad**　**excited**

　　_____

　　_____

5. How many times do I have to tell you? Leave me alone.
　　sad　**mad**　**excited**

　　_____

　　_____

6. It's such a beautiful day. Let's go outside.　**happy**　**mad**　**afraid**

　　_____

　　_____

Writing Traits: Word Choice

Word choice activities assist students in learning how to use vivid, colorful, and dynamic words to enrich their writing. (Use the Word Choice poster on page 82 to display in your classroom.)

Descriptive Words

For very young children, word choice activities focus on describing people or objects using appropriate adjectives and adverbs.

1. Begin by writing the story below on chart paper. (Be sure to include the blank lines.)

   The _____ monkeys were in the trees. They made _____ noises. They moved _____ from branch to branch.

2. Read the story aloud and ask the questions below.
   - Do you know the color of the monkeys?
   - Do you know if the noises were loud or quiet?

3. Explain that we can't answer those questions because the story doesn't include describing words.

4. Read the story again, line by line.

5. Ask the students to suggest words to write in the blanks. When the lines are filled, read the story again.

6. Compare the two versions.

7. Have students complete page 83 for further practice.

Description

1. Explain that when writing, we can use describing words, but we can also include details.

2. Read the first story version below.

Version #1

My mom was busy cleaning the house. I could tell I shouldn't bother her. She was in a hurry.

Ask the following questions:

- Why is Mom cleaning the house?
- How did the boy/girl know he/she shouldn't bother her?

Explain that by including more details, we help the reader to understand the story better. Read the second version of the story.

Description *(cont.)*

Version #2

My *dad's boss was coming to dinner. When I got home*, Mom was cleaning the house. She was rushing from room to room. She had a serious look on her face. I could tell I shouldn't bother her.

---

3. Compare the two versions and draw student's attention to the extra sentences telling why Mom was cleaning and the expression on her face. For more practice, have students complete page 84.

Feeling Words

1. Students often use the same words to express feelings in a story—*sad*, *mad*, *bad*, and *glad*.

2. Help your students add more colorful feeling words by reviewing alternatives for these feelings (see below).

3. Have students practice using these words by completing page 85.

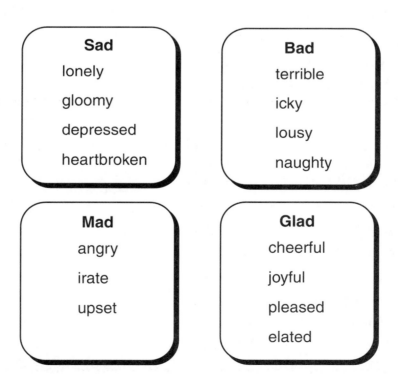

Sad

lonely

gloomy

depressed

heartbroken

Bad

terrible

icky

lousy

naughty

Mad

angry

irate

upset

Glad

cheerful

joyful

pleased

elated

Writing Traits: Word Choice *(cont.)*

"Said" Words

One way to assist children with the word choice writing trait is to provide new words to use instead of the word "said."

1. Demonstrate the need for this by reading aloud a paragraph that includes an exchange of dialog.

2. Read the passage again and replace words like *replied, exclaimed, shouted,* with the word "said." (See below.)

Version #1

Angela called out to her mom, "I'm over here!"

"Oh, there you are, honey," replied her mother. "I thought I had lost you."

"You should have seen the clowns that were in the parade," giggled Angela.

"Were they funny?" asked Mother.

"They were! You must see them perform."

"I'm not sure we have time, Angela."

"You have to," she insisted.

Version #2

Angela said to her mom, "I'm over here!"

"Oh, there you are, honey," said her mother. "I thought I had lost you."

"You should have seen the clowns that were in the parade," said Angela.

"Were they funny?" said Mother.

"They were! You must see them perform."

"I'm not sure we have time, Angela."

"You have to," she said.

---

3. Draw students' attention to the difference between the two paragraphs and how the change of words adds interest.

4. Distribute student copies of pages 86 and 229. Review the synonyms for "said" and have the students use these words to complete page 86.

Word Repetition

Repeating words in a story is a simple way to add interest.

1. Write the sentences below on the chalkboard.
   - It was such a sad movie.   • It was a happy day.

2. Ask the students to identify the adjective in each sentence.

3. Then write the sentences again, showing what happens when the descriptive words are repeated.
   - It was such a sad, sad movie.   • It was a happy, happy day.

4. Have students review stories they have written to find descriptive words that could be repeated to add more emphasis.

5. Distribute page 87 to students for further practice of the skill.

Word Choice

The word choice trait focuses on the use of rich language and descriptive writing to impress or move the reader.

☑ descriptive words

☑ strong verbs

☑ rich language

Adding Descriptive Words

Add description to each story. Write a descriptive word on each line.

1. Shelly wore a _____ dress. It had _____ ruffles.

   It was her birthday. She was excited to see her _____ friends

   at the party.

2. It was Max's turn to bat. He was nervous. You could tell by looking at his

   _____ face. He walked _____ to the plate.

   He swung the bat _____. It was a homerun!

3. I heard _____ music in the hallway. It made me feel

   _____. Who was playing the piano? I walked

   _____ down the hall to find out.

4. The _____ child played in the yard. She wore

   _____ shoes and a _____ dress. Her

   _____ face told me that she was happy.

5. My dad and I swam in a river. The water was _____ and

   _____. It felt _____ when it touched my

   skin. As I swam, I could see the _____ sun in the sky.

6. That was a _____ movie. The people looked

   _____ and _____. My favorite part was

   when the _____ man saw his _____ son for

   the first time.

Details, Details

Rewrite each story below. Use descriptive words and more sentences to add detail.

1. The dog was barking. He wouldn't stop. Something was bothering him.

_____

_____

_____

_____

2. Grandmother came to visit. The kids were all excited. She had something for them.

_____

_____

_____

_____

3. The room was decorated for the party. It looked pretty.

_____

_____

_____

_____

4. The car drove by. It scared me.

_____

_____

_____

_____

5. I didn't realize I was so tired. As soon as I stopped to rest, I fell asleep.

_____

_____

_____

_____

How Do You Feel?

Write a feeling word on each line. Choose words from the word box.

1. Sally's friends all went home. She felt _____.

2. Baley was in a good mood. She was very _____.

3. I hurt my friend's feelings. Now I feel _____.

4. When the sky is cloudy, I feel _____.

5. I felt _____ when I broke my favorite toy.

6. Mom was _____ with her son's work.

7. Don't get _____. We'll work it out.

8. I hate snakes. They are _____.

9. I rushed through my work and did a _____ job.

10. Kelly was jumping up and down. She was _____ about going to the beach.

Word Box

upset	elated	terrible	icky
cheerful	heartbroken	pleased	lousy
gloomy	lonely		

"Said" Words in Action

Use the words on page 229 to assist you in completing the sentences below.

1. "Stop hitting me!" _____ Katie.

2. Joe _____, "That was the funniest thing!"

3. "I hate doing homework," _____ Kevin.

4. "Please can we have an extra recess?" _____ the class.

5. "Hurry! You're going to miss the bus," _____ Alex.

6. "You must come with us," Mother _____.

7. "Give me that pencil!" _____ Courtney.

8. Donny _____, "This is such a great day!"

Word Repetition

Underline the descriptive word in each sentence. Then rewrite the sentence, repeating the descriptive word. The first one has been done for you.

1. Sit down in the green grass.

   Sit down in the green, green grass.
   _____

2. I love to swim in the cool water.

   _____

3. The hot sun beat down on the park bench.

   _____

4. We have such a long way to walk.

   _____

5. That was a silly thing to do.

   _____

6. We could hear the soft sound of the breeze.

   _____

7. We're going to have a fun time.

   _____

8. She blew a big bubble.

   _____

Writing Traits: Sentence Fluency

Sentence fluency focuses on sentence variety, length, and the musical quality of words when they are placed near each other. The activities below will help your students recognize the rhythm and flow of language and use this skill in their own writing. (Use the Sentence Fluency poster on page 89 to display in your classroom.)

Varying Sentence Length

1. Explain to your students that it is important to write sentences with different lengths when writing stories. When all sentences are the same length, the story sounds boring.

2. Provide the following example by reading the passages below.

Version #1

We went to the park. It was nice. We played on the swings. We ran around. It was a perfect day. We had fun.

Version #2

We went to the park last Saturday. We had a nice time. We played on the swings and ran around in the grass. It was such a perfect day and we had lots of fun.

---

3. Ask the students to compare the two stories and share the differences they notice.

4. Then write the two story versions on chart paper and compare the actual lengths of the sentences to show how sentence length makes a difference.

5. Distribute student copies of page 90 for beginning writers and page 91 for more advanced writers and have them complete the page to reinforce the skill.

Demonstrating Sentence Fluency

As mentioned above, sentence fluency focuses on varied sentence length and rhythm. The books below can be used to demonstrate this skill.

- *If I Were in Charge of the World and Other Worries* by Judith Viorst
- *Time for Bed* by Mem Fox
- *The Sign of the Seahorse* by Graeme Base
- *Alexander, and the Terrible, Horrible, No Good, Very Bad Day* by Judith Viorst
- *The Night Before Kindergarten* by Natasha Wing

Fluency Modeling

Since sentence fluency can be a difficult skill for young children, you may need to model the thought processes for writing in this way.

1. Demonstrate sentence fluency by writing a story in front of the class.

2. As you develop the story yourself, talk to yourself about how the sentences sound and how the ideas can be combined to create longer sentences.

3. You might even want to pose questions and encourage the students to assist you in writing the story.

Sentence Fluency

This trait refs to the rhythm and flow of the writing.

☑ pleasing to the ear

☑ reader flows through the story

☑ varied sentence length

Adding Words

Practice writing longer sentences. Rewrite each sentence, adding at least two more words. The first one has been done for you.

1. I like the beach.

   I like the beach because I have fun there.

2. I saw a bird.

3. I had fun.

4. We went to the zoo.

5. I love pizza.

6. My friend is nice.

7. Don't ride your bike so fast.

8. That game is fun.

9. I love reading books.

10. She was happy.

Sentence Length

Rewrite each short story below. Change the sentences so they are different lengths.

1. Sally is my dog. I love her. She has brown fur. Her fur is curly. I like to play with her. She sleeps with me. Sally is my friend.

_____

_____

_____

_____

2. The carnival was fun. I went with my family. We saw animals. We went on rides. I ate too much. I got sick. I had fun anyway.

_____

_____

_____

_____

3. I like pizza. It is my favorite food. Do you like it? My favorite topping is pepperoni. My dad took us out for pizza. It was good. I hope we go again.

_____

_____

_____

_____

Writing Traits: Conventions

If writing does not follow the standard form in conventions, it can be very difficult to read and understand. The conventions writing trait focuses on spelling, grammar, paragraphing, and punctuation. (Use the Conventions poster on page 93 to display in your classroom.)

Editing for Spelling

For young children, editing can be a difficult task and should be carefully guided and focused.

1. Begin by explaining to students the importance of spelling correctly.

2. Tell them that even book authors have to carefully check their work and have other people (called editors) check their spelling as well.

3. To make this task more manageable for your children, focus on the spelling of some commonly used words (see the word cards on pages 94-99), such as *the, and, what, they, could,* etc.

4. Display these words in a prominent location in the classroom and tell students that they will edit classmates' writing for the spelling of these words.

5. Pair students together and have each share a recently written story. Encourage them to read the story together, looking for any of the target words.

6. Instruct them to verify correct spelling or make changes as needed.

7. Add new and more difficult words to the list as students become more proficient editors.

8. Provide each student with a copy of page 100 for further practice.

Editing for Punctuation

Just like the editing of spelling, editing for punctuation can be a daunting task for young children.

1. Begin by having children edit only for capital letters or one or two end marks and then add more editing tasks as they increase their abilities as editors.

2. To introduce editing for punctuation, review the use of end marks and capitalization with your students (see pages 101–102 for skill practice).

3. Then introduce basic editing marks that are used to indicate mistakes. For example, when a word needs to be capitalized, the first letter is underlined three times. When a sentence needs an end mark, a ^ points to the place needing an end mark and the punctuation is written above it.

   - i like going to school.   • This is a fun activity   • how are you today

4. Encourage students to practice using these editing marks.

5. When they are ready for more of a challenge, introduce other marks (see page 242 of the Writer's Notebook).

6. Provide each student with a copy of page 103 for further practice.

Conventions

Conventions refer to the mechanics of the written work. The focus is on spelling, grammar, use of paragraphs, use of capital letters, and punctuation.

- ☑ spelling

- ☑ grammar

- ☑ use of paragraphs

- ☑ use of capital letters

- ☑ punctuation

High-Frequency Word Cards

about	after
again	always
and	because
been	before
both	came
carry	come

High-Frequency Word Cards

could	does
done	down
eight	everything
find	found
four	friend
goes	going

High-Frequency Word Cards

have	here
into	just
kind	know
laugh	light
little	live
look	made

High-Frequency Word Cards

make	many
most	much
never	new
nothing	now
once	one
over	own

High-Frequency Word Cards

please	put
question	read
right	said
saw	say
some	soon
thank	the

High-Frequency Word Cards

them	their
there	under
use	very
want	wear
were	where
which	yours

Editing for Spelling

See the words in the box below. Edit the sentences for the correct spelling of these words by writing the correct spelling above each. Hint: Some sentences have more than one misspelled word.

they	what	would	have	about
come	eight	friend	goes	laugh

1. It wood be nice to see you.

2. It's abut time to go.

3. Jayda is my best frend.

4. How much money do you hav?

5. Alex gos to my school.

6. Did you see wat thay gave me?

7. Wat time did you comb in?

8. That joke made me laf.

9. There are ate fish in the tank.

10. I don't know wat to do.

Editing for Punctuation

The sentences below are missing end marks. Edit each sentence and show which ones need periods, question marks, or exclamation marks.

- Use a **period** at the end of a sentence that tells something.
- Use a **question mark** at the end of a sentence that asks something.
- Use an **exclamation mark** at the end of a sentence that shows excitement.

1. How many do you have

2. Can you help me with my homework

3. You are a good student

4. Mrs. Clay is my favorite teacher

5. How are you today

6. Watch out

7. Oh no, I broke it

8. I got a new kitten

Editing for Capital Letters

The first word in a sentence must always begin with a **capital letter**. Find the letters that should be capitalized and write three lines below each. Then write the word above it using a capital letter.

1. it's time for school.

_____

2. when is your birthday?

_____

3. tony is on the playground.

_____

4. did you see the thunderstorm?

_____

5. summer is my favorite time of year.

_____

6. let me help you with that.

_____

7. kelly, what are you doing?

_____

8. i can't wait for vacation!

_____

Up for a Challenge?

Put your editing skills to work. Edit the sentences below for **capital letters**, **punctuation**, and **spelling**. (Use the spelling words below.) Then rewrite each sentence correctly.

| after | thank | because | does | live | know | many |

1. what are you doing aftr the game

_____

2. tank you for helping me

_____

3. Did you no that I'm on the team

_____

4. I have too meny hamsters

_____

5. how many pets dos she have?

_____

6. She helped me becuz she's nice

_____

7. let's go to the game together

_____

8. Where do you live?

_____

Writing Traits: Presentation

Presentation involves adding visual elements to written work in order to increase its appeal. (Use the Presentation poster on page 107 to display in your classroom.)

Illustrations/Mounting

Allow students to present their edited written work with flair.

1. Mount each child's story on the lower portion of a large sheet of construction paper.

2. Then have the child illustrate a scene from his or her story on the upper portion of the construction paper.

3. You can also have the student create a decorative border for the illustration by sponge painting or drawing colorful geometric shapes around the edges.

Accordion Book

This is a simple way for students to create booklets for displaying completed stories.

1. To create a booklet, you will need one sheet of white and one sheet of colored construction paper.

2. Cut each sheet of construction paper in half vertically and discard half of each sheet.

3. Position the colored strip of paper horizontally on a desktop.

4. Squeeze a trail of glue along one long edge of the paper.

5. Place the white strip of paper atop the glue and press to secure. Allow the glue to dry.

6. Then accordion-fold the paper three times to make a booklet.

7. The student writes his or her story on the lower (colored) portion of each section and draws an illustration on the upper (white) portion of each section. (Writing pages that will fit the size of the book are provided on page 108.)

Graduated-Page Book

A unique way to display a child's story is in a booklet with graduated pages.

1. To do this, cut four sheets of construction paper (assorted colors) using the following dimensions:

   Page 1: 9" x 5.5"
   Page 2: 9" x 6.5"
   Page 3: 9" x 7.5"
   Page 4: 9" x 8.5"

2. Stack the pages from shortest to longest and then staple them together.

3. After creating a decorative cover on the first page, the student writes sections of the story and corresponding illustrations on the remaining pages. (Writing pages that will fit the pages of the book are provided on pages 109 and 110.)

Writing Traits: Presentation *(cont.)*

Computer-Generated Illustrations

Adding computer-generated graphics is a delightful way for students to add illustrations to their completed written work. There are many forms of computer graphics and programs that can be used, including the following:

- children's graphic program (such as *KidPix*)
- word-processing program with a drawing tool (such as *Microsoft Word*)
- word-processing program with clip art (such as *Microsoft Word*)

The children can create their graphics and then print them out to include in handmade booklets or add story text to the graphics for electronic versions of the stories.

Imported Computer Graphics

Images used to adorn students' finished written work can be downloaded from the Internet.

PC Users:

1. Right-click on the selected image. A small dropdown menu will appear.
2. Drag to "Save Picture As."
3. You will be asked to designate the location where you want the image stored on your computer.

Macintosh Users:

1. Click on an image while holding down the Control key. A dropdown menu will appear.
2. Drag to "Download Image to Disk."
3. You will be asked to designate the location where you want the image stored on your computer.

Once the image is saved, it can be copied and pasted into the electronic file or printed out and pasted into a booklet.

Dioramas

Short stories or reports can be displayed in a small three-dimensional diorama.

1. Duplicate a copy of page 111 for each student.
2. Have each student use construction paper, markers or crayons, and glue to create the setting of the story on the upright blank side of the diorama.
3. Each child writes the story text on the writing lines provided on the diorama template.
4. Cut on the dotted line. Be sure not to cut further than the center dot.
5. Take the two flaps on either side of the cut line and overlap them so the flap with the writing lines is on top. A triangular shaped diorama will be the result.
6. Glue the overlapping flaps together.

Writing Traits: Presentation *(cont.)*

Pop-Up Story Display

Here's a fun way for students to display stories and illustrations.

1. Duplicate a copy of page 112 for each student.

2. Fold the paper on the bold line (the dotted lines should be on the outside of the fold).

3. Cut on the two short dotted lines.

4. Halfway open the page and, using your index finger, "pop" forward the cut section.

5. Refold the page and crease the fold lines once again.

6. Make the pop-up display sturdier by gluing a sheet of construction paper to the back of the display. (Be sure not to glue down the cut section.)

7. The student writes his or her story text on the provided lines and glues a cutout illustration to the pop-up section.

Story/Report Cube

Here's a fun way for students to present their stories.

1. Duplicate a copy of page 120 for each student.

2. The student writes a part of the story on sections 1, 2, 4, and 5 of the cube. (See numbers on the sections for proper sequence.)

3. The student draws pictures to accompany the story on sections 3 and 6.

4. Help students assemble their cubes by folding on dotted lines and gluing the tabs.

Shapes and Mysterious Shapes

Inspire story writing with this creative activity.

1. For seven different shape booklets, use the patterns on pages 113–119.

2. For mysterious shapes, provide each student with copies of pages 121 and 122.

3. The student colors and cuts out the desired shapes and then glues them onto page 121 to form an object or creature.

4. The student then colors a background in the box.

5. Finally, the student writes a story about the picture on the lines.

If You Could See What I See

Your students' imaginations will soar with this creative writing activity.

1. Begin by providing a copy of page 123 for each student.

2. The student cuts out the glasses pieces and assembles them.

3. Provide construction paper, markers, and assorted embellishments to decorate the glasses.

4. Tell the students to pretend that these are glasses that do magic things when worn.

5. Instruct each child to write a story about the magic glasses.

Presentation

The final trait focuses on the visual elements of the writing.

☑ handwriting

☑ neatness

☑ format

☑ illustrations

☑ visual aids

Accordion Book Writing Pages

Graduated Page Booklet Writing Pages

Graduated Page Booklet Writing Pages

Diorama Template

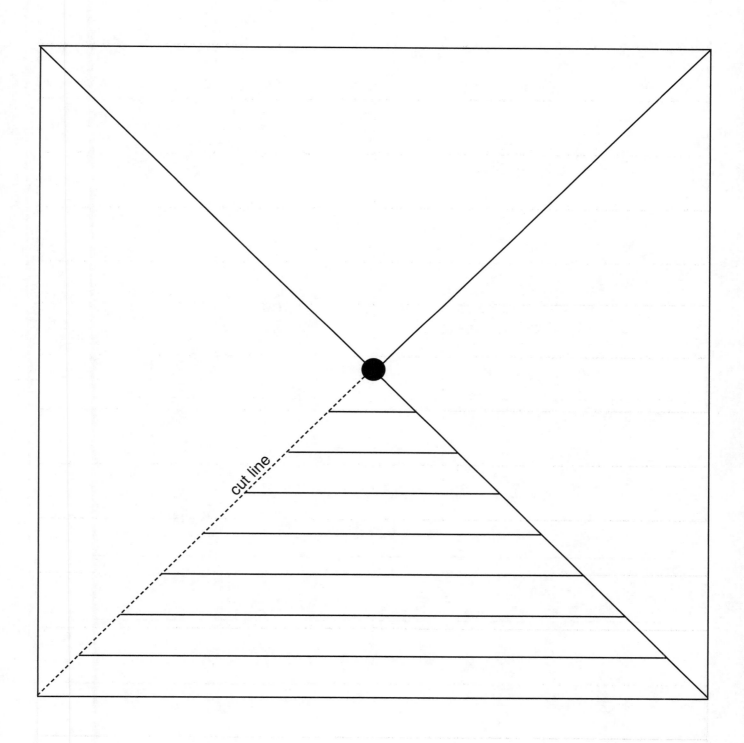

cut line

Writing Traits: Presentation *(cont.)*

Pop-Up Display Template

cut
line

cut
line

fold line

_____

_____

_____

_____

Dog Shape Booklet

Rocket Shape Booklet

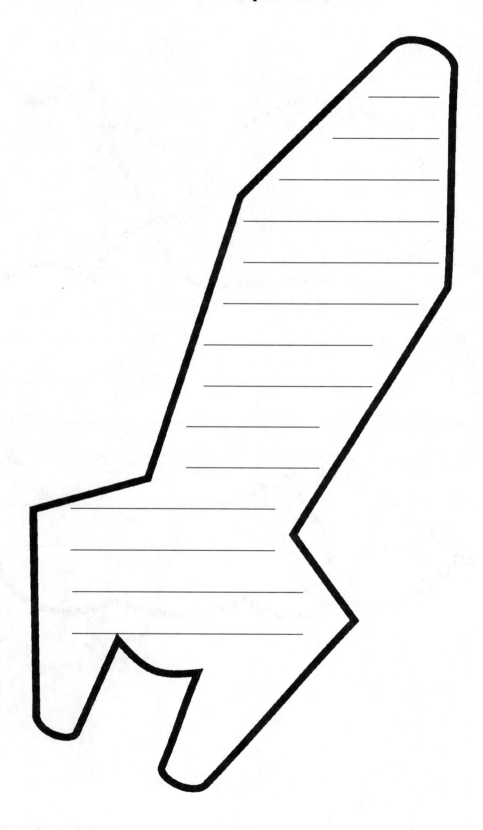

Cloud Shape Booklet

Paper Doll Shape Booklet

Monster Shape Booklet

Truck Shape Booklet

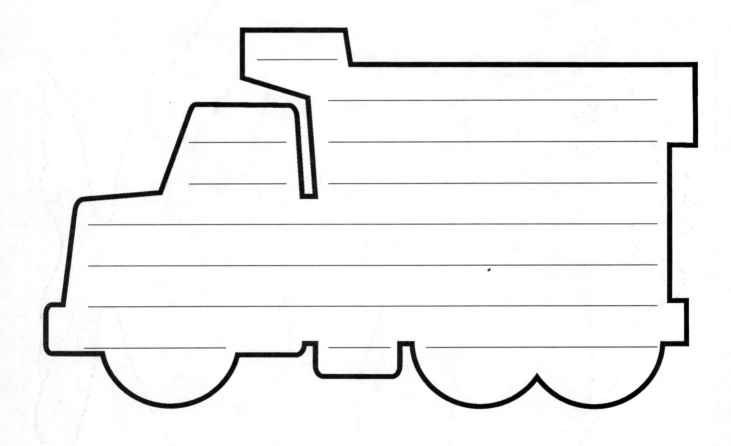

Fish Shape Booklet

Story/Report Cube

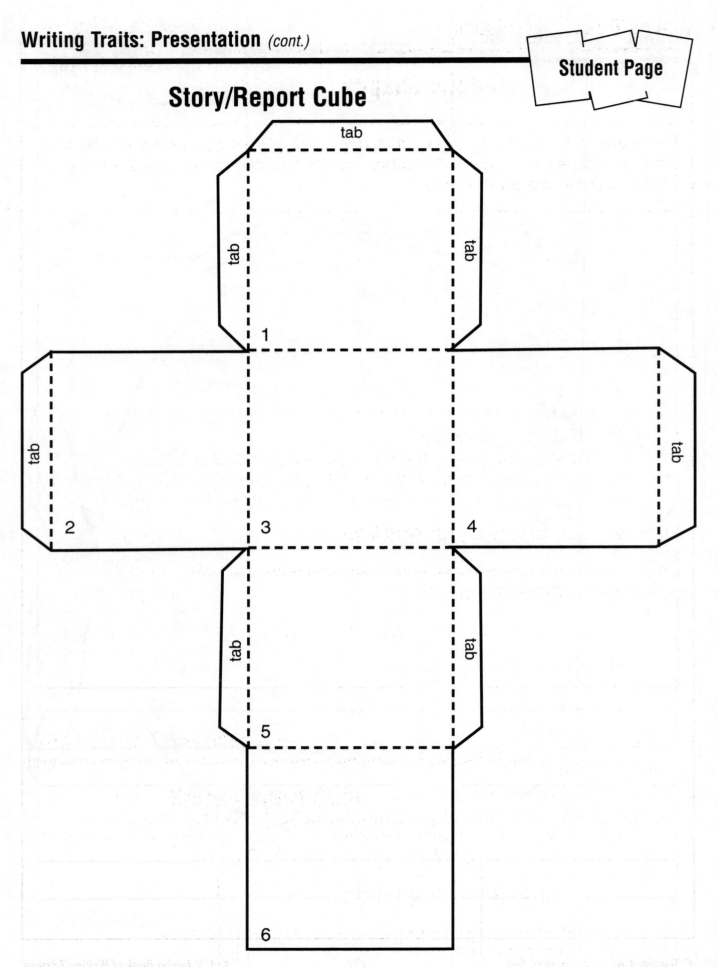

Mysterious Shapes

Color and cut out a few shapes from page 122. Create an object or creature with the shapes and glue it in the box. Color a background. Write a story about your picture on the lines.

Mysterious Shapes *(cont.)*

If You Could See What I See

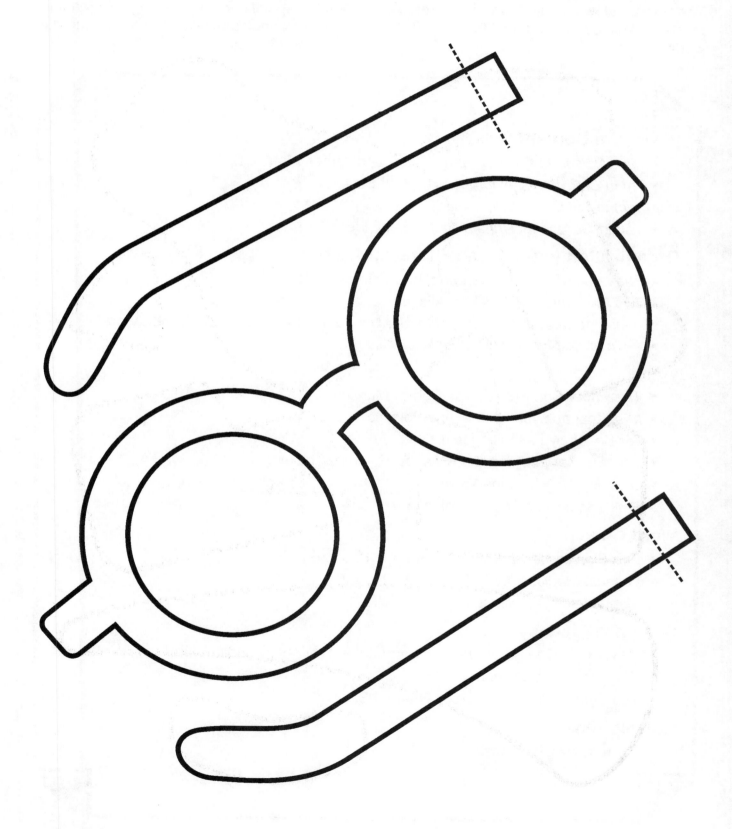

Writing Traits in Literature

The books below contain many excellent examples of the specific traits of writing. By reading these books aloud to your children, you will provide vivid examples of how they are featured in writing.

Ideas and Content
- *Miss Nelson Is Back* by Harry Allard and James Marshall
- *I'm in Charge of Celebrations* by Bird Baylor
- *Jumanji* by Chris Van Allsburg
- *Wilfrid Gordon McDonald Partridge* by Mem Fox

Organization (strong transitions and sequence)
- *The Legend of the Bluebonnet* by Tomie dePaola
- *Two Bad Ants* by Chris Van Allsburg
- *Alexander and the Terrible, Horrible, No Good, Very Bad Day* by Judith Viorst
- *A Chair for My Mother* by Vera B. Williams

Voice
- *The Paper Bag Princess* by Robert Munsch
- *Mrs. Katz and Tush* by Patricia Polacco
- *Tar Beach* by Faith Ringgold
- *The Teacher from the Black Lagoon* by Mike Thaler
- *Sleeping Ugly* by Jane Yolen
- *Pink and Say* by Patricia Polacco

Word Choice
- *The Sign of the Seahorse* by Graeme Base
- *Possum Magic* by Mem Fox
- *Many Luscious Lollipops* by Ruth Heller

Sentence Fluency
- *If I Were in Charge of the World and Other Worries* by Judith Viorst
- *Slugs* by David Greenberg
- *The Sign of the Seahorse* by Graeme Base

Conventions
- *Yo! Yes?* by Chris Raschka

Word Play

Your children will get a kick out of these wordplay activities. Schedule a time each day to have fun with language.

Idioms

1. Learning about idioms is an entertaining way to improve children's knowledge of language. The following is a list of common idioms you can discuss with your students.

Idiom		Figurative Meaning
frog in the throat	→	hoarse voice
fork in the road	→	road splits into two
under the weather	→	feeling ill
got up on the wrong side of the bed	→	in a bad mood
raining cats and dogs	→	raining really hard

2. Discuss the literal and figurative meanings of the idioms.

3. Then have each student select an idiom and have him or her illustrate both the literal and figurative meanings.

4. As an added activity, use pages 129–131 to create a learning center. Duplicate and cut apart the cards. The student then determines whether each picture is depicting the literal or figurative meaning of the idiom.

More about Idioms

Your students will have fun determining literal and figurative meanings of idioms.

1. Review with your students the meaning of the word *idiom*. Explain that an idiom is a phrase that has a "figurative" meaning when it is typically used in our language, but it can have a funny literal meaning. For example: *It's raining cats and dogs*. In our language this means that it's raining really hard, but literally it would mean that cats and dogs are falling from the sky.

2. If your students are ready for a challenge, distribute student copies of page 132.

3. To complete the page, a student looks at the picture and idiom in each box and then writes two sentences on the lines. The first sentence should explain the figurative meaning of the idiom, and the second sentence should explain the literal meaning.

Example: Turn right at the fork in the road.

> **Sentence 1:** When the road splits into two, take the road on the right.

> **Sentence 2:** When you see a fork lying in the road, turn right.

Similes

1. Explain to your students that writers often compare things using similes. For example:

   Her eyes were as blue as the sky.

   His hair was brown like chocolate.

2. Draw students' attention to the fact that similes usually use the words *like* or *as*. Have students practice creating their own similes using pages 133 and 134.

Metaphors

Like a simile, a metaphor also compares two different things but without using the words *like* or *as*. For example:

   Her hair was sunlight.

   The blanket was cotton.

1. Show the children how to create a metaphor by selecting a noun, such as *kitten*, and writing it on the chalkboard.

2. Then ask yourself aloud:

   —What comes to mind when I think of a kitten?

   —Kittens are furry.

   —Kittens look like little fluff balls.

3. Create a metaphor by writing on the chalkboard:

   The kitten was a ball of fluff.

4. Have students continue to practice making metaphors using pages 135 and 136.

Onomatopoeia

Onomatopoeia refers to words that sound like the noise made by certain objects or actions, such as *meow, moo, bang,* and *buzz.*

1. Ask the students to think of other examples of onomatopoeia as you write their responses on chart paper.

2. Tell the students that onomatopoeia is used to add interest to stories. Read the following example aloud.

   > Callie and Jordan walked to school in the rain. Big fat drops *pitter-pattered* on their umbrellas. *Splish, splash, splish, splash* went their feet in the puddles. Callie slipped and fell. *"Ouch!"* she cried.

3. Draw students' attention to the use of sounds in the story. Reread the story without the sound words and compare the two versions.

4. Divide the students into small groups to write stories using onomatopoeia. (Encourage them to use page 235 in the Writer's Notebook for assistance.) Allow the students to share their stories with the class.

5. For more practice using onomatopoeia, have students complete pages 137 and 138.

Personification

Personification is used to add interest to writing. It is a writer's way of assigning human characteristics to objects or animals. For example:

The fox gave a sly smile and ran away. (A fox wouldn't really smile like a person would.)

The tree held out its arms against the wind. (A tree doesn't actually have arms.)

1. To write personification, have students think of verbs and adjectives that describe human actions, such as dance, cough, love, grab, tired, or embarrass.

2. List parts of a human body, such as arms, legs, heart, brain, mouth, etc. List the students' responses on chart paper.

3. Once these lists are compiled, name an object, such as a car.

4. Ask the students to determine whether the car will be thought of as being male or female.

5. Then give them an example of personification, such as:

   The tired car sputtered and coughed as she came to a stop.

6. Draw students' attention to the fact that the words *tired*, *coughed*, and *she* are typically used to describe people, but in this case are used to describe a nonliving thing.

7. Have students continue practice using personification by completing pages 139 and 140.

Hink Pinks

Hink Pinks are riddles that involve critical thinking and rhyming skills. For example: An unhappy father would be a *Sad Dad*. See the list below for a few others.

- A not-so-nice vegetable is a *Mean Bean*.
- A distant automobile is a *Far Car*.
- A goofy flower is a *Silly Lily*.

1. To make a Hink Pink, it is easiest to begin by listing adjectives, such as *happy, sad, mean, red, black, tall, short*, etc., on chart paper.

2. Select an adjective and then try to think of nouns that rhyme with it. For example, the word *tall* rhymes with such nouns as *ball, hall, mall, stall*, and *wall*.

3. Next, determine which noun and adjective will be used for the Hink Pink, such as Tall Stall.

4. Now, it's time to create a clue that means the same thing. Ask the students what another word for *tall* is, such as *high* or *big*. Another way to say *stall* is *booth*. So, the Hink Pink riddle would be something like this:

   What is a high booth? (It's a "Tall Stall.")

5. Continue in this manner creating more Hink Pinks as a class. Then allow students to create their own, using page 141.

Alliteration

Alliteration is a phrase or sentence that contains several words with the same beginning consonant sound. For example:

Billy bought a bunch of bright blue balloons.

1. Introduce students to many examples of alliteration by sharing some you have created or read the book *Animalia* by Graeme Base.

2. Draw students' attention to the words that begin with the same beginning letter, but point out that some small words do not have to begin with that letter.

3. Create some alliterations together by brainstorming subjects, verbs, and adjectives that have the same beginning letter. Write these on chart paper.

4. Then ask the students to put some of the words together to make sentences.

5. Have them practice creating their own alliterations using pages 142 and 143.

Imagery

Good writers use descriptions that assist the reader with "picturing" the setting of the story.

1. Demonstrate this by reading the two sentences below.

The butterfly flew past me.

Floating on the breeze, a small, orange butterfly gently passed me.

2. Ask the students to compare the two sentences, deciding which one provides a picture of the scene.

3. Draw their attention to the fact that the first sentence answers the following questions:
   - What flew by?
   - What did it pass?

4. The second sentence answers many more questions.
   - What flew by?
   - How did it fly?
   - What did it look like?
   - What did it pass?
   - How did it pass by?

5. Have the students practice creating imagery by looking at landscape photos from magazines. Instruct the student to ponder the following questions:
   - What colors do you see?
   - Are the colors bright or faded?
   - Are there people or animals in the picture? How do they look?
   - What actions might take place in that setting (*wind blowing, birds singing*)?
   - What words could be used to describe these actions?

6. Instruct the students to use the answers to the questions to write their own imagery. For additional practice, provide students with copies of page 144.

Idiom Cards

Cut it out!

Cut it out!

It's time to hit the hay.

It's time to hit the hay.

I've got my eye on you.

I've got my eye on you.

Idiom Cards

I'm feeling under the weather.

I'm feeling under the weather.

Zip your lip!

Zip your lip!

Don't blow your top.

Don't blow your top.

Idiom Cards

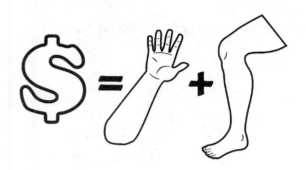

It cost an arm and a leg.

It cost an arm and a leg.

He's all bent out of shape.

He's all bent out of shape.

It's raining cats and dogs.

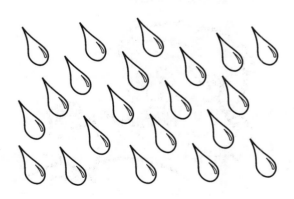

It's raining cats and dogs.

Defining Idioms

Look at the idiom cards your teacher shows you. Write two sentences defining the idiom. The first sentence should explain the *figurative* meaning of the idiom and the second sentence should explain the *literal* meaning.

Example: Turn right at the fork in the road.

Figurative: When the road splits into two, take the road on the right.

Literal: When you see a fork lying in the road, turn right.

1. It's raining cats and dogs.

Figurative: _____

Literal: _____

2. My brother is a pain in the neck.

Figurative: _____

Literal: _____

3. I'm so hungry, I could eat a horse.

Figurative: _____

Literal: _____

4. Let's keep in touch.

Figurative: _____

Literal: _____

5. You're the apple of my eye.

Figurative: _____

Literal: _____

Similes

Similes are used to compare things. Similes usually use the words "like" or "as."

For example:

> Her eyes were *as* blue *as* the sky.
> His hair was brown *like* chocolate.

Complete the similes below.

1. The star was as _____ as _____.

2. The airplane is as _____ as _____.

3. The blanket was like a _____.

4. My kitten is like a _____.

5. The river was as _____ as _____.

6. The crash was as _____ as _____.

7 The dog was like a _____.

8. The baby was as _____ as _____.

9. The balloon is as _____ as _____.

10. The pizza was as _____ as _____.

Similes

Read each word below. Think about something that comes to mind to compare it with. Write a simile using each word.

1. teeth _____

_____

2. wind _____

_____

3. clouds _____

_____

4. mountain _____

_____

5. rainbow _____

_____

6. snow _____

_____

7. racecar _____

_____

8. eyes _____

_____

9. candy _____

_____

10. leaf _____

_____

Metaphors

A **metaphor** compares two different things **without** using the words *like* or *as*. For example:

> Her hair was sunlight in my eyes.
>
> The snow was a blanket on the road.

Create a metaphor using the following steps.

1. Write a noun (a naming word) on the line below.

   _____

2. Ask yourself:

   What does this word make me think of? _____

   What does it feel like?_____

   Does it have a particular sound or taste?_____

   What does it do?_____

3. Use the answers above to create a metaphor. Write your metaphor below. (Remember not to use the words *like* or *as*.)

   _____

   _____

   _____

   _____

   _____

   _____

   Write a few more metaphors.

   _____

   _____

   _____

   _____

Using Metaphors and Similes in Writing

Create a **metaphor** below.

_____ was a circus.

Complete the **similes** below.

_____ as a _____

_____ as a _____

Write the name of two story characters below.

_____   _____

Write a sentence telling about the setting of a story.

_____

Use the information above to write a story. Be sure to use the metaphor and both similes in your story.

_____

_____

_____

_____

_____

_____

_____

_____

_____

_____

Listen to This!

Onomatopoeia refers to words that sound like the noise made by certain objects or actions, such as *meow*, *moo*, *bang*, and *buzz*.

Write a sound for each word below.

1. bird _____

2. car _____

3. wind _____

4. rain _____

5. bell _____

6. lion _____

7. dog _____

8. bee _____

9. horse _____

10. sneeze _____

11. train _____

12. laugh _____

Can You Hear Me?

Write a sentence using **onomatopoeia** for each word or phrase.

1. truck

   _____

2. cat

   _____

3. eating soup

   _____

4. wind

   _____

5. cow

   _____

6. skidding tires

   _____

7. getting hurt

   _____

8. door

   _____

9. explosion

   _____

10. baby crying

   _____

Personification

Complete each sentence below using **personification**. Remember that personification involves giving human qualities to nonhuman objects.

1. The alarm clock told me _____

_____.

2. My dog said _____

_____.

3. The piano sang _____

_____.

4. The leaves danced _____

_____.

5. The breeze whispered _____

_____.

6. The cat tip-toed _____

_____.

7. The snow kissed _____

_____.

8. The blanket hugged _____

_____.

More Personification

Personification is used to add interest to writing. It is a writer's way of assigning human characteristics to objects or animals.

Think of adjectives and verbs that describe people. Write a sentence about each animal or object below using personification.

1. dog

   _____

2. lake

   _____

3. duck

   _____

4. star

   _____

5. train

   _____

6. moon

   _____

7. door

   _____

8. mouse

   _____

Hink Pinks

Hink Pinks are riddles that involve critical thinking and rhyming skills. For example: An unhappy father would be a *Sad Dad*. See the list below for a few others.

- A not-so-nice vegetable is a *Mean Bean*.
- A distant automobile is a *Far Car*.
- A goofy flower is a *Silly Lily*.

Follow the steps below to create a Hink Pink.

1. Make a list of adjectives (describing words) on the lines below.

   _____   _____

   _____   _____

   _____   _____

   _____   _____

2. Choose one of the adjectives and then write a list of nouns (naming words) that rhyme with it.

   _____   _____

   _____   _____

   _____   _____

3. Choose the adjective and noun you will use and write each below.

   _____   _____

4. Think of a synonym for each word and write them below.

   _____   _____

5. Write your Hink Pink below.

   A _____ _____ is a _____ _____

Tie Up Your Tongue!

Practice using **alliteration**. For each letter or blend below, write four or five words that have the same beginning sound.

Example:

C *cat, caught, candy, cave* _____

F _____

L _____

P _____

S _____

T _____

Dr _____

Pl _____

Sl _____

On each line below, write a sentence using alliteration.

1. _____

2. _____

3. _____

Alliteration

Remember that **alliteration** uses several words in a sentence that begin with the same letter. Words like *on, and, in,* and *the* can also be used in the sentence. Write alliterations on the lines below.

1. _____

2. _____

3. _____

4. _____

5. _____

Draw a picture of your favorite alliteration below.

Imagery

Imagery involves writing with description so that a reader can picture the scene or characters.

Example:

> **No imagery:** *The frog hopped.*
>
> **Imagery:** *The little, green frog hopped off the lily pad and into the clear water.*

Rewrite each sentence below using imagery.

1. The clock struck three.

   _____

2. A car passed the house.

   _____

3. Music was playing.

   _____

4. I could smell the pizza.

   _____

5. She ran home.

   _____

6. There was a waterfall.

   _____

Now, think about your favorite place to be. Using imagery, write a paragraph on another sheet of paper to describe this place in detail.

Test Yourself!

Write the figurative meaning of each idiom.

1. I'll keep an eye on you.

_____

2. Zip your lip!

_____

Write an **S** beside each simile. Write an **M** beside each metaphor.

3. _____ She was as slow as a snail.

4. _____ The man was a mountain.

5. _____ The baby's skin was like silk.

6. _____ I'm as cold as ice.

7. _____ Happiness is a good friend.

For each word below, write an example of onomatopoeia.

8. frog _____

9. door _____

10. owl _____

Write a **P** beside each example of personification. Write an **A** beside each example of alliteration.

11. _____ Can you calm the crying kid?

12. _____ Four friendly ferrets found food.

13. _____ The guitar sang sweetly.

14. _____ The clock announced that it was time for lunch.

Songwriting

Music is an engaging incentive for student writing. Try these activities and watch your students blossom into songwriters.

Rewriting Nursery Rhymes

1. Teach students to identify the sounds of beginning letters by having them participate in a singing/songwriting activity.

    (Sung to the tune of "London Bridge.")
    Bessy bird lives in a barn, in a barn, in a barn.
    Bessy bird lives in a barn, and she is happy.
    She likes to eat bacon, bacon, bacon.
    She likes to eat bacon, and it tastes good.

2. Draw students' attention to the words that begin with the /b/ sound. Ask them to identify the kind of animal in the song (*a bird*), the name of the bird (*Bessy*), where Bessy lives (*a barn*), and what she eats (*bacon*). Sing the song with the students several times to learn the words and the pattern of the song.

3. Write the following headings on chart paper: *Names, Animals, Homes, Food.* Tell students that they will now create a new verse to the song using a different beginning letter sound, such as /p/. Begin with the category "Names" and ask students to think of names that begin with the /p/ sound. Write the students' contributions on the chart paper to create a list.

4. Continue in the same manner, brainstorming words for animals, homes, and food that begin with /p/. See below.

Names	Animals	Homes	Food
Patty	pig	pool	peaches
Peter	panda	pond	pears
Polly	poodle	package	pizza

5. Next, write the following verse frame on the chart paper:

    _____ _____ lives in a _____, in a _____, in a _____.
    _____ _____ lives in a _____, and she/he is happy.
    She/He likes to eat _____, _____, _____.
    She/He likes to eat _____, and it tastes good.

6. Invite students to select a name, an animal, a home, and a kind of food to add to the frame. When the blanks are filled, review the new words to the song and sing it together several times.

7. Have students create their own song verses using the verse frame on page 148.

Rhyming to Music

Rhyming is a natural skill when used in the context of singing songs. This activity engages children by teaching rhyming concepts through music. This lesson can be adapted for beginning writers.

1. Begin the lesson by teaching students to sing the song "A-Hunting We Will Go." (See the words below.)

    Oh, a-hunting we will go, a-hunting we will go.

    We'll take a little fox and put it in a box

    and then we'll let it go.

2. Ask the students to identify the two words that sound the same (*fox* and *box*). Continue to sing the song with the following phrases to replace the second line. As you sing the song, pause for the second rhyming word and allow the students to sing the word they think rhymes. This should be easy and fun for students.

    We'll take a little whale and put it in a pail

    We'll take a little frog and put it on a log

    We'll take a little fish and put it on a dish

3. Allow students to sing the song together several more times using both the original lyrics and the three new verses.

4. Ask students to brainstorm other animals that could be used in the song. List these animals on chart paper. Then ask the students to think of words that rhyme with each animal name. For example:

    snake: lake, cake, rake

    bear: hair, dare, chair

    cat: hat, mat

5. Next, write the following verse frame on chart paper.

    Oh, a-hunting we will go, a-hunting we will go.

    We'll take a little _____ and put it in a _____

    and then we'll let it go.

6. Invite students to choose one of the animal names from the brainstorming list and one of the rhyming words. Write these words in the blanks of the verse frame.

7. For additional practice, instruct students to make their own lists of animal names and rhyming words.

8. Provide each student with the verse frame on page 149. Ask each student to create two or three verses to the song by writing pairs of rhyming words in the blanks.

9. Once they have completed their verses, gather the students together and allow them to share them. Sing the verses together as a class.

Song Template

_____ _____ lives in a _____, in a _____, in a _____.

_____ _____ lives in a _____, and she/he is happy.

She/He likes to eat _____, _____, _____.

She/He likes to eat _____, and it tastes good.

- -

_____ _____ lives in a _____, in a _____, in a _____.

_____ _____ lives in a _____, and she/he is happy.

She/He likes to eat _____, _____, _____.

She/He likes to eat _____, and it tastes good.

- -

_____ _____ lives in a _____, in a _____, in a _____.

_____ _____ lives in a _____, and she/he is happy.

She/He likes to eat _____, _____, _____.

She/He likes to eat _____, and it tastes good.

A-Hunting We Will Go Template

Oh, a-hunting we will go, a-hunting we will go.

We'll take a little _____ and put it in a _____

and then we'll let it go.

Oh, a-hunting we will go, a-hunting we will go.

We'll take a little _____ and put it in a _____

and then we'll let it go.

Oh, a-hunting we will go, a-hunting we will go.

We'll take a little _____ and put it in a _____

and then we'll let it go.

Extending Vocabulary

Working with children on vocabulary helps them to make their story writing more interesting.

Conversational Vocabulary

In order for children to internalize new vocabulary words they must hear them used often and in different ways. One way to remind students of the meanings of new words is to use them interchangeably with familiar words. For example, a teacher might say, "Be sure to write an adjective, a describing word that tells about the character." By pairing a new word with its synonym, your children will begin to recognize the use and meaning of the new word.

Interesting Words

Encourage your students to begin a collection of new words.

Materials

- copy of page 151 for each student
- children's book
- pencil

1. Distribute a copy of page 151 for each student. You might want to have each student keep the page in a special folder.

2. The student records a new word in the first column.

3. In the second column, the student writes where he or she found the word (a book, through conversation, etc.).

4. Next, the student writes the definition of the word.

5. In the last column, the student writes how the word was originally used.

6. Provide extra sheets of page 151, so students can continue collecting words throughout the year.

New Words in Print

Reading aloud to children has many benefits that relate to all areas of reading and writing development. The reading of stories can also help children to develop increased vocabulary. This can be done quite naturally in a daily read-aloud time in class. When new words are encountered, adults can pause to discuss them, asking the following questions:

- Have you heard this word before?
- What do you think it means?
- Do you know of other words that sound the same or have similar parts?
- Listen to the way the word is used in a sentence. Does this give you clues to the word's meaning?

While the discussion of new words during story time is important, it is also important to maintain the enjoyment of the story. Discuss new words, but don't discuss so many that the students lose track of the story line.

Interesting Words

New Word	Where I Found It	Definition	How It Was Used

Letter Writing

These lessons provide students with the skills necessary to write friendly letters, business letters, and letters expressing opinions.

Friendly Letter Recipients

1. Explain to students that letters can be sent to people we know and people we don't know.

2. Letters sent to those we know are called friendly letters.

3. Ask the students to think about people to whom they might write friendly letters, such as friends, family members, teachers, and neighbors.

4. Display the following two letters:

Dear Mom,

You are very special to me. You help me with my homework. You always take care of me. I love it when you read to me at night.

Love,
Melody

Dear Sir:

I am writing to ask if my class could visit your store for our field trip. We are learning about workers in our community, and we would like to talk to you about your business.

Sincerely,
Jesse Hanes

---

5. Ask the students to determine which letter is a friendly letter and have them explain why.

6. Draw their attention to the different format of each letter and explain that they will learn the formats for friendly and business letters.

Friendly Letter Format

1. On a sheet of chart paper, write a friendly letter in proper format.

2. Read the letter aloud to the students and draw their attention to the position of the date, greeting, body, closing, and signature. Point out that the body of the letter is indented.

3. Spend a few minutes discussing each part of the letter, asking questions such as:
   - Why do you think this is called *the greeting*?
   - Why would we call this part of the letter *the body*?
   - Why do you think we would call this *the closing*?

4. Have the students practice labeling the parts of a friendly letter by completing page 156.

5. For further reference, have students use the Friendly Letter Template on page 236.

Business Letters

1. Begin the lesson by asking students why a person might write a business letter. What kind of person would receive this kind of letter?

2. Explain that business letters are written to people we don't know very well, people we have never met, or people in authority. They are usually written about concerns or requests, or to give information.

3. As a class, make a list of people to whom they might write business letters and the things they might write to them about.

4. Provide each student with a copy of page 157. For each featured person, the student writes topics he or she would write about in a letter. For example, a letter to the principal might be about unsafe playground equipment or bullies on the playground.

Business Letter Format

1. Explain to the students that the format of a business letter is different from a friendly letter.

2. Display a business letter on chart paper and show the students the different positioning of the date, closing, and signature.

3. Also, point out that a business letter includes the name and address of the person and does not use an indented body.

4. Have students practice writing and labeling business letters by completing page 158.

5. For further reference, have students use the Business Letter Template on page 237.

Writing Greetings

1. Tell students that usually letters begin with the same greeting—*Dear*. However, not all letters have to begin with that greeting.

2. Display the list below to show different greetings for friendly and business letters.

Friendly-Letter Greetings	*Business-Letter Greetings*
Dear _____,	Dear _____:
Hi _____,	Dear Sir:
Dearest _____,	Dear Madam:
	To Whom It May Concern:

Greetings *(cont.)*

3. Discuss why certain greetings should only be used in friendly letters and certain ones only in business letters. For example, why wouldn't we write "To Whom It May Concern" when writing to a friend? Why wouldn't we write "Hi, Mr. President"?

4. Draw students' attention to the use of commas in friendly-letter greetings and colons in business-letter greetings.

5. Have students complete page 159 to practice selecting appropriate greetings for different people.

Closings

1. Ask students to tell how a letter should end.

2. Explain that when we close a letter, we use a closing such as "Your friend" or "Sincerely." A closing should be selected based on the relationship the writer has with the recipient. For example, a letter to a parent might use "Love" in the closing. It might be strange to use "Love" when closing a letter to someone you don't know.

3. Have the children brainstorm common closings as you list them on the chalkboard. See the list below.

- Love,
- Your friend,
- Sincerely,
- Truly yours,
- Yours truly,
- Sincerely yours,
- Fondly,
- Your student,

4. Discuss each of the closings. Then read the list of people below and ask the children to identify which closing would be appropriate to use in a letter to each one.

- teacher
- sister
- parent
- principal
- school librarian
- sports coach
- governor
- friend

5. Draw students' attention to the punctuation used in closings and emphasize that the first word is capitalized and the second word is not.

6. For further practice, have students complete pages 160 and 161.

7. Page 238 of the Writer's Notebook provides further reference for students.

Addressing a Letter

1. Distribute addressed envelopes and junk mail to the students.

2. Ask them to identify the name and address of each person. Draw their attention to the placement of the recipient's address and the sender's address.

3. Ask the children to tell why it is important to properly address an envelope. Be sure to mention that the return address is important, so the letter can be returned to you if it cannot be delivered for some reason.

4. Write a sample name and address on the chalkboard. Point out that the name goes on the first line, the street address is on the second line, and the city, state, and zip code are on the third line. Be sure to draw their attention to the punctuation, capitalization, and abbreviations.

5. Distribute copies of pages 162 and 163 for further practice.

Persuasive Letters

1. Begin the lesson by explaining that sometimes people write letters to persuade people to do something. When we persuade, we try to get someone to do something or to change his or her mind.

2. Divide the children into small groups and provide each group with a set of Telling and Persuading cards (page 164).

3. Each group should read the cards and determine whether the words are being used to share information or to persuade.

4. Explain that there are words or phrases that can be used effectively to change a person's mind, such as the following:

   - I suggest that . . .
   - I recommend that . . .
   - I think you should . . .
   - You might like to try . . .

5. As a class, choose something you would like to persuade another class to do, such as recycling paper or assisting you with cleaning up trash on the playground.

6. Invite students to contribute to the letter by making a request to the other class and offering information and reasons to convince the class to join you.

7. After writing the letter, have students identify the words and sentences used that might persuade the class to take action.

8. Have students practice writing persuasive sentences by completing page 165.

Friendly-Letter Format

Use this page to write a letter to someone you know. When you are finished, cut out the labels and glue them in the proper places.

Dear _____,

date

body   signature

greeting   closing

Business Letter Topics

Write topics for letters to each person below.

The President

_____

_____

Principal

_____

_____

Restaurant Owner

_____

_____

Newspaper Editor

_____

_____

Make a list of other people to whom you could write a business letter. Write the topic of the letter you might write.

Person	**Topic**
_____	_____
_____	_____
_____	_____
_____	_____

Business Letter Format

Write a business letter to your principal. Cut and paste to label the parts of the letter.

_____   ☐

_____   ☐

_____

_____

Dear _____,   ☐

_____

_____

☐

_____

_____

_____

_____

_____,   ☐

_____   ☐

date	greeting	closing

name and address	body	signature

Select Your Greeting

Imagine that you will write a letter to each person listed below. Determine the greeting you would use in the letter and write it on the line. Be sure to use correct punctuation. Use the box below to help you.

1. best friend

   _____

2. parent

   _____

3. business woman

   _____

4. brother or sister

   _____

5. principal

   _____

6. grandparent

   _____

Greetings

Dear _____,	Dear Sir:
Hi _____,	Dear Madam:
Hello _____,	To Whom It May Concern:
Dearest _____,	

Select a Closing

For each person listed below, write an appropriate closing. Be sure to use correct punctuation and capitalization.

1. parent _____

2. friend _____

3. aunt _____

4. teacher _____

5. principal _____

6. neighbor _____

7. store owner _____

8. coach _____

Closings

Love,	Yours truly,	With love,
Your friend,	Sincerely yours,	Your student,
Sincerely,	Fondly,	

Writing Closings

Rewrite each closing below, using the correct capitalization and punctuation.

1. love, _____

2. your Friend, _____

3. sincerely. _____

4. Yours Truly, _____

5. Sincerely Yours: _____

6. fondly _____

7. with love, _____

8. Your Student; _____

Can you think of other closings you could use? Write them below.

_____

_____

_____

_____

State Abbreviations

Look at the chart of states and their abbreviations.

Alabama—AL	Louisiana—LA	Ohio—OH
Alaska—AK	Maine—ME	Oklahoma—OK
Arizona—AZ	Maryland—MD	Oregon—OR
Arkansas—AR	Massachusetts—MA	Pennsylvania—PA
California—CA	Michigan—MI	Rhode Island—RI
Colorado—CO	Minnesota—MN	South Carolina—SC
Connecticut—CT	Mississippi—MS	South Dakota—SD
Delaware—DE	Missouri—MO	Tennessee—TN
Florida—FL	Montana—MT	Texas—TX
Georgia—GA	Nebraska—NE	Utah—UT
Hawaii—HI	Nevada—NV	Vermont—VT
Idaho—ID	New Hampshire—NH	Virginia—VA
Illinois—IL	New Jersey—NJ	Washington—WA
Indiana—IN	New Mexico—NM	West Virginia—WV
Iowa—IA	New York—NY	Wisconsin—WI
Kansas—KA	North Carolina—NC	Wyoming—WY
Kentucky—KY	North Dakota—ND	

Write the abbreviation for each state below.

1. Alaska _____

2. Wyoming _____

3. North Carolina _____

4. Oklahoma _____

5. Colorado _____

6. New Mexico _____

7. Washington _____

8. Indiana _____

9. Delaware _____

10. Nevada _____

11. California _____

12. Ohio _____

13. Arizona _____

14. Montana _____

162

Addressing an Envelope

Rewrite each name and address, correcting mistakes with capitalization and punctuation. Be sure to abbreviate each state.

james chang
2275 south hudson
denver, colorado 80234

_____
_____
_____

mike jesson
19847 court street
chino hills, california 91709

_____
_____
_____

jody heinrich
13221 rolling hills lane
dallas, tx 75240

_____
_____
_____

amy settle
854 higby road
utica new york 13035

_____
_____
_____

randy hoffner
8843 north forest lane
flagstaff, arizona 86004

_____
_____
_____

shirley chen
12875 east valley road
chandler az 85224

_____
_____
_____

pam wilburn
843 south street
redmond, wa 98052

_____
_____
_____

Telling or Persuading?

1. Our dog is cute. She is black and white. She wears a red collar. She loves to chew on her toys. I love it when she sleeps beside me.

2. Cats are the best pets to have. They have cute faces and soft fur. They don't need baths. They don't make messes and they are cuddly to sleep with.

3. We have a new car. It's white and has two back seats. My whole family can fit in it. I don't have to be squished anymore. I love our new car.

4. Have you ever tried to ski? Skiing is the best sport. It takes some time to learn, but it's really fun. You really should learn to ski. I know you'd like it.

5. My favorite season is winter. I love to watch snow fall gently from the sky. I like the sound of my feet crunching in the snow. It is so beautiful to see clumps of snow hanging from the trees. Winter is lovely!

6. We should all pitch in to help clean up the playground. Our playground should be a nice place to play, but it is filled with trash. If every class spent a few minutes each day picking up trash, we could have it cleaned up in no time. Please help us make the playground a nice place to be.

Persuade Me

For each activity listed below, write two reasons that will persuade someone to try it.

1. learn a new hobby

_____

_____

2. read a book

_____

_____

3. go to the fair

_____

_____

4. get a certain kind of pet

_____

_____

5. try a new food

_____

_____

6. learn a new sport

_____

_____

Making Book Reports

There are many kinds of book reports in traditional and not-so-traditional formats. This section will provide ideas for your students to make exciting book reports.

Traditional Book Report

A traditional book report includes the basics of a story—title, author, illustrator, and story summary. It's important that you review each of these elements and even practice writing summaries. (See Writing a Summary on page 39.) Duplicate copies of the traditional book report on page 167.

Character Journal

A character journal requires that the student assume the role of a main character in a story. The student then writes a journal entry from the character's point of view. Duplicate copies of page 168 for students. This page provides question prompts to assist students in writing about story events from characters' perspectives.

I Learned a Lesson

Books can often teach us lessons. Provide an example of this by reading a short story (perhaps a selected fable from Aesop) that teaches a lesson. Ask the students to identify the lesson taught in the story and which character learned this lesson. Then ask them if they can apply this lesson to their lives. How would they handle the situation if it happened to them? Duplicate page 169 for students and have them write about lessons learned in stories they have read.

Storybook/Slide Show

You can use page 170 to help students plan a storyboard presentation. If you have the Technology and Software, a Powerpoint presentation can be dramatic.

Planning an Oral Book Report

Book reports don't always have to be written. An oral report is an important activity. Explain that when presenting an oral report, a person should tell the title of the book, the author, the main characters, and important story events. The person can also tell about his or her favorite part and whether or not he or she recommends that others read the book. This can seem like a daunting task, so provide each student with a copy of the planning sheet on page 171. Encourage students to practice their oral reports before presenting to the class.

Traditional Book Report

Name _____

Book Title _____

Author _____

Illustrator _____

Story Summary

_____

_____

_____

_____

_____

_____

Illustrate your favorite part of the story.

Character Journal

Pretend that you are a character in the story you read. Write a journal entry telling about some events in the story. Use the questions below to help you.

- Who are you? _____
- What is your age? _____
- Who else is in the story? _____
- What happened to you in the story? _____
- How did you feel about this? _____

Write a journal entry as if you are this character.

Book Title: _____

Author: _____

Illustrator: _____

Dear Diary,

_____

_____

_____

_____

_____

_____

Draw a picture of the character.

I Learned a Lesson

Books can often teach lessons. These lessons help us in our own lives. Think about the lessons learned in a book you read and answer the questions below.

Book Title: _____

Author: _____

• What lesson is taught in this story?

_____

_____

_____

_____

_____

• Who learned the lesson?

_____

_____

• What happened to the character, and what did the character do?

_____

_____

_____

_____

_____

_____

_____

• What would you do if the same thing happened to you?

_____

_____

_____

_____

_____

PowerPoint Storyboard

Directions: Plan your slide show by sketching where you want text and pictures to appear. Number the slides in the squares on the bottom right side of the slide. Ask for additional pages if needed.

• • • • • • • • • • •

Planning an Oral Book Report

Use this page to help you plan an oral report about a book you read. Read through this page to remember what you wrote. Practice saying your report out loud before presenting to the class.

- The book I read was

  _____

- The author of the book is

  _____

- The book was about the following main character(s)

  _____

  _____

  _____

- In the story (discuss events)

  _____

  _____

  _____

  _____

- My favorite part of the story was

  _____

  _____

  _____

  _____

- I do (do not) recommend this book because

  _____

  _____

  _____

Simple Research Report

Writing a research report might seem like an advanced skill, but young children can write short reports with a bit of assistance.

Select a Topic

Selecting a manageable topic is important. If a topic is too broad, it will be difficult to handle in a short report. For example, a child might choose the topic desert animals. This is a very broad topic because there are so many different kinds. Explain to the students that narrowing the topic to a specific desert animal, such as the Gila monster, is a better topic. Assist your students in selecting and narrowing topics using page 173.

Questioning the Topic

Once a topic is selected, a student should brainstorm questions he or she would like to know about it. For example:

- Where do Gila monsters live?
- What do they look like?
- What do Gila monsters eat?
- How big are they?
- Are they poisonous?

Duplicate page 174 for each student. This page will assist students in creating questions to direct their research.

Writing Note Cards

Believe it or not, your students can collect information about their topics using note cards.

1. Duplicate three copies of page 175 for each student and have them cut the note cards apart.
2. Explain that when a fact is found, information about the topic and the source where it is found is recorded on a card.
3. The student writes the title and author of the book, page where the fact was found, and the fact written in the student's own words.
4. To assist your students with this task, do a group fact-finding by reading aloud a book about a topic such as elephants.
5. When a student hears an interesting fact, he or she raises a hand.
6. Then, as a class, complete a note card, including title, author, page number, and paraphrased fact.

Writing the Report

Once students have collected six facts about their topics, explain to them that they will use these facts to write a report. Show them how to sort the facts into a logical sequence. The following list might assist in sequencing facts about an animal:

- What is the animal?
- Where does it live?
- How does it look?
- What is interesting about it?

Have students write their final reports on copies of page 176.

Selecting a Topic

Think about a topic that interests you. Be sure the topic is not too big. For example, *ocean* is a big, broad topic that is hard to research, but *starfish* is an easier (narrower) topic to tackle.

Read each topic below. Write a narrowed topic beside each.

1. bugs _____

2. forest animals _____

3. sports _____

4. dogs _____

5. careers _____

6. weather _____

7. planets _____

8. zoo animals _____

Write your topic below.

_____

Can your topic be narrowed? Write a narrowed topic below.

_____

Questioning the Topic

Once you have a topic, think of the questions you have about it. For example, if your topic is prairie dogs, your questions might be ones like these:

- Where do prairie dogs live?
- What do they look like?
- What do they eat?
- How big are prairie dogs?
- What is special about them?

Write the name of your topic. Then write several questions that you have about your topic.

Topic:

_____

Questions:

1. _____

2. _____

3. _____

4. _____

5. _____

Use these questions to guide your research.

Writing Note Cards

Title and author of book:

_____

Page number where fact was found: _____

Write the fact using your own words:

_____

_____

_____

Title and author of book:

_____

Page number where fact was found: _____

Write the fact using your own words:

_____

_____

_____

Title and author of book:

_____

Page number where fact was found: _____

Write the fact using your own words:

_____

_____

_____

Writing the Report

Title of Report

Draw a picture about your topic.

Poetry

These activities will enable you to teach your students that poetry is fun and creative.

Creating Rhymes

While not all poems contain rhyming words, rhyming is important for some forms of poetry, so have some fun creating rhymes.

1. Make this a playful, informal activity by saying a series of rhyming words, such as pot, got, trot.
2. Ask the students to contribute other words that sound the same.
3. You might want to list these words on chart paper so students can see that the words have similar endings.
4. Explain that these words are rhyming words because they end with the same sound.
5. You can also refer them to pages 247-249 for lists of word families.
6. For more practice with making rhymes, have students complete page 180.

Couplets

Teach students to use their rhyming skills to create couplets.

1. Explain that a couplet is made up of two lines that rhyme, such as these:

> I looked up in the light blue sky
>
> and thought I saw a cherry pie.

2. Ask the students to identify the rhyming words (*sky* and *pie*). Give them some couplet starters and have them try to fill in the blanks. See below.

> Do you want to have some fun?
>
> Let's go skip and walk and _____!
>
> Let's all go outside to play
>
> Until the sun has gone _____.

3. If students have trouble completing the couplets, brainstorm lists of rhyming words and let them select a word that is appropriate for the couplet.
4. For additional practice creating couplets, have students complete page 181.

Cinquain

Cinquain poems are very simple for young children.

1. Explain that these poems have specific patterns to follow.

> Line 1: noun
>
> Line 2: two adjectives describing the noun
>
> Line 3: three verbs about the noun
>
> Line 4: a sentence or phrase about the noun
>
> Line 5: a renaming noun

Cinquain *(cont.)*

2. Provide an example of a cinquain poem, such as the following:

Clouds

White, fluffy

Floating, drifting, blowing

They look so soft.

Cotton

3. Duplicate page 182 for each student and have them each create a poem using this format.

Shape Poems

1. These are fun because the text of the poem is written in the shape of the topic.

2. A poem about ice cream would be written in the shape of an ice-cream cone.

3. Shape poems can, but do not need to, rhyme.

4. For practice, have student write poems in the shapes on page 183.

I Feel Poems

This poetry style is easy for young children to create.

1. Ask the students to describe how they feel right now.

2. Encourage them to use words that address their feelings.

3. Next, review similes with your students (see the section on Word Play, page 126) and tell them that they will create poems using similes about themselves.

4. Distribute copies of page 184 to each student to complete.

Name Poems

1. To write a name poem, a child writes his or her name vertically and then writes a word or phrase that begins with each letter in the name. See the examples below.

J	Joyful	**D**	Digging in the garden
E	Energetic	**O**	Opening closets to steal shoes
N	Nice	**G**	Good for snuggling
N	Natural		
I	Interesting		
F	Fun		
E	Educated		
R	Realistic		

2. Have the students begin by creating poems using their first names. Then have them choose other words to write about.

3. Duplicate copies of page 185 for students to use.

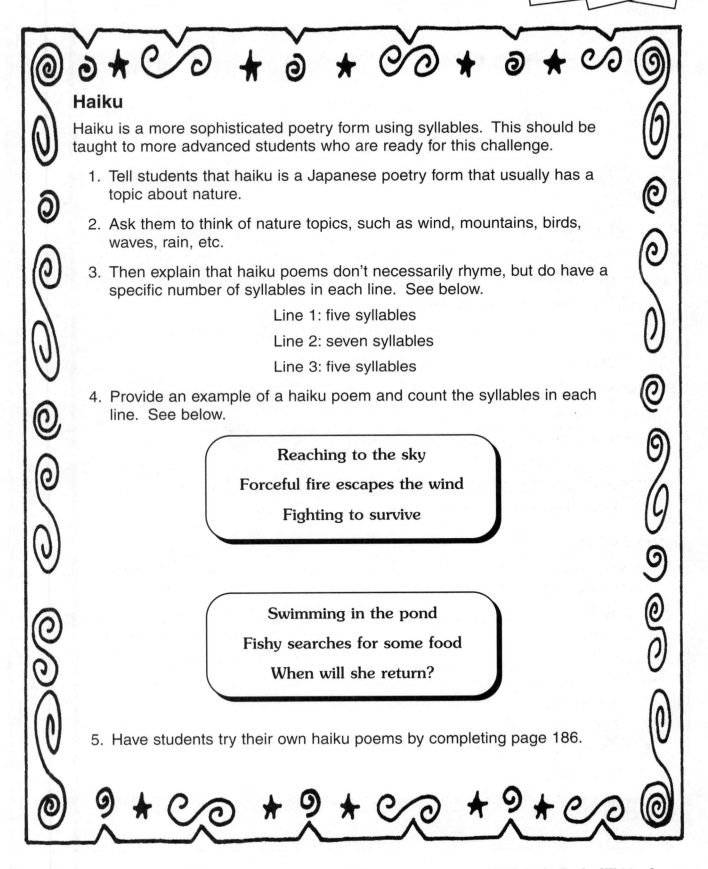

Haiku

Haiku is a more sophisticated poetry form using syllables. This should be taught to more advanced students who are ready for this challenge.

1. Tell students that haiku is a Japanese poetry form that usually has a topic about nature.

2. Ask them to think of nature topics, such as wind, mountains, birds, waves, rain, etc.

3. Then explain that haiku poems don't necessarily rhyme, but do have a specific number of syllables in each line. See below.

Line 1: five syllables

Line 2: seven syllables

Line 3: five syllables

4. Provide an example of a haiku poem and count the syllables in each line. See below.

Reaching to the sky

Forceful fire escapes the wind

Fighting to survive

Swimming in the pond

Fishy searches for some food

When will she return?

5. Have students try their own haiku poems by completing page 186.

Creating Rhymes

For each word below, write a list of rhyming words.

1. black _____

2. hot _____

3. sun _____

4. see _____

5. slide _____

6. slow _____

7. red _____

8. might _____

9. play _____

10. toy _____

11. green _____

12. make _____

Couplets

A couplet is made of two lines that rhyme, such as the following:

> Do you want to have some fun?
>
> Let's go skip and walk and run!

Try to make a couplet for each set of rhyming words below.

(try, fly)

_____

_____

(see, tree)

_____

_____

(sun, fun)

_____

_____

(toy, boy)

_____

_____

(cap, tap)

_____

_____

Cinquain

Cinquain poems have five lines. Each line has a specific pattern.

  Line 1: noun
  Line 2: two adjectives describing the noun
  Line 3: three verbs about the noun
  Line 4: a sentence or phrase about the noun
  Line 5: a renaming noun

Here's an example:

Clouds
White, fluffy
Floating, drifting, blowing
They look so soft.
Cotton

Try to create a cinquain of your own, using one of the topics in the box below.

_____
noun

_____   _____
adjective   adjective

_____   _____   _____
verb   verb   verb

_____
phrase or sentence

_____
renaming noun

Topic Ideas

a sport	a kind of weather	a kind of food
a kind of insect	a hobby	a subject in school
a family member	a pet	a best friend

Shape Poems

Inside each shape, write a poem about the object represented by that shape.

I Feel Poem

Complete the similes to create a poem about yourself.

I feel as happy as _____.

I feel as silly as _____.

I feel as light as _____.

I feel as worried as _____.

I feel as jumpy as _____.

I feel as frightened as _____.

I feel as shy as _____.

I feel as angry as _____.

I feel as excited as _____.

I feel as strong as _____.

Name Poems

To write a name poem, write your name vertically in the boxes below. Then write a word or phrase that begins with each letter in your name. See the example below.

A	Always nice
B	Boy who likes soccer
E	Everything is funny

Haiku

Haiku is a Japanese poetry form that usually has a topic about nature. Think of five nature topics and write them below.

_____   _____   _____   _____   _____

Follow the pattern below to write a haiku poem about a nature topic.

Line 1: five syllables

Line 2: seven syllables

Line 3: five syllables

Swimming in the pond (five syllables)

Fishy searches for some food (seven syllables)

When will she return? (five syllables)

_____ (five)

_____ (seven)

_____ (five)

Descriptive Writing

Descriptive writing describes a person, place, thing, event, memory, or an idea. This type of writing can be descriptive, reflective, or exploratory in nature and in themes. The student writes descriptions about a scene, a character, a person, an animal, noises, etc. The descriptions might come from an event observed by the student, an experience the student had, or an idea the student created. This domain includes writing that often appears in the following:

- journals
- poetry
- folktales
- myths
- tall tales
- stories
- songs
- plays
- fables

Sentence Frames

1. Write the following sentence frames on the chalkboard.
    - My favorite color is _____.
    - I have _____ brothers and _____ sisters.
    - Apples taste _____.
    - My favorite flavor of ice cream is _____.

2. Read each frame with the class and discuss the words that could be used to complete the sentence.

Describing Colors

1. Have your children describe how different colors make them feel or what they make them think of. For example, "Red is cheerful." "Red tastes like cherry pie."

2. Try this activity with a variety of colors—blue, yellow, green, purple, etc.

Replacing Common Verbs

1. Write several sentences on the chalkboard, using common verbs.

2. Ask the children to replace the underlined verbs with stronger verbs—that is, ones that are more specific or descriptive. For example, "The boy walked home," could be changed to, "The boy strolled home."

Describe a Person

Have each child describe a friend or family member, using descriptive words to tell about the person's appearance and/or behavior.

Adjectives

At the primary level, students use adjectives to get beyond the simplest of sentences and add interest to their writing.

1. To introduce adjectives, show the students a picture and ask them to tell you about it.

2. Record their descriptive responses on chart paper.

3. Tell the students that the words written on the chart paper are called adjectives. Explain that adjectives are words that are used to describe or tell about something. Stories are more interesting when the authors describe things. This helps us to form mental pictures of the story.

4. Brainstorm a long list of adjectives with the class and write them on chart paper. (Be sure to draw students' attention to the adjectives lists on page 250 in the Writer's Notebook.)

5. Next, divide a sheet of bulletin-board paper into four sections. Write one sentence in each section:

Section 1: The cat is eating.	**Section 2:** The black cat is eating.	**Section 3:** The big, black cat is eating.	**Section 4:** The big, furry, black cat is eating.

6. Ask volunteers to draw pictures to illustrate the sentences in each section. Explain that the words added to each sentence are adjectives. Also point out how the pictures became more interesting and detailed as adjectives were added.

Similes

1. Explain that similes are used to describe objects creatively.

2. Instead of saying that the day-old bread is hard, a person could say it is "as hard as a rock." This gives a reader a better idea of just how hard it is.

3. Have students practice this as a class, using the following simile frames.

   • The moon is as _____ as _____.

   • The sun is as _____ as _____.

   • A baby is as _____ as _____.

   • A ladybug is as _____ as _____.

   • A night sky is as _____ as _____.

   • Music is as _____ as _____.

4. For more activities using similes, see pages 133, 134, and 233.

Descriptive Writing *(cont.)*

Strong Verbs

Using strong verbs in descriptive writing is one way authors show, rather than tell, their readers and increase interest in their writing. With this activity, help your students increase their vocabulary by practicing strong, specific, colorful verbs that they can use in the descriptive writing.

1. Begin the lesson by showing the students a children's thesaurus. Explain that a thesaurus is a book of words arranged in alphabetical order like a dictionary, only a thesaurus shows synonyms for words rather than definitions.

2. Read a few entries from the thesaurus as examples, making sure that the students understand the meaning of *synonym*.

3. Now discuss and record on chart paper some examples, such as *eat* (chew, gulp, devour) *walk* (plod, saunter, shuffle), *said* (blurted, mumbled, chirped), and *look*. Brainstorm other words that mean almost the same thing as the verbs on the chart but describe the actions more specifically. Add these words to the chart.

4. Be sure to have the children refer to the synonyms lists in the Writer's Notebook for other word alternatives.

Dramatizing Verbs

After the children learn about strong verbs, have them participate in a fun game.

1. Duplicate, cut apart, and distribute the verb cards on pages 194 and 195.

2. In turn, have each student act out the verb on his or her card.

3. Ask other students to try to guess the word.

4. Draw students' attention to the subtle differences between the actions of similar words, such as *ate, gobbled,* and *nibbled.*

Adverbs

At the primary level, students use adverbs to tell when and how something happened.

1. Write when and how at the top of a sheet of chart paper as column headings.

2. Ask students to name words that tell when, such as *first, before, after, during, now, then.*

3. Write them under the heading *when.*

4. Do the same for the word *how.* Some words that tell how are the –ly words, such as *quickly, slowly, happily, badly, cheerfully,* and *sadly.* Tell them that adverbs often end in –ly.

5. Duplicate and cut apart the strips on pages 196 and 197.

6. In turn, students select a strip and dramatize it for the class.

7. Classmates attempt to guess what is being dramatized, including the adverb describing the action.

8. For further practice, have students complete page 198.

Sentence Frames

Use descriptive words to complete the sentences below.

1. The sky is _____ and _____.
                 adjective   adjective

2. The _____ dog _____ _____.
          adjective   verb (action)   adverb (describe the verb)

3. The _____ boy _____ to the _____.
          adjective   verb (action)   place

4. I want a _____ bowl of _____ _____.
             adjective   adjective   food

5. The teacher's voice sounded _____.
                                       adjective

6. He studied _____ for _____ days.
                 adjective   number

7. Her _____ hair blew _____ in the wind.
          adjective   adverb (describe the verb)

8. The _____ boy tripped on the _____ rock.
          adjective   adjective

Describing Colors

Use your senses to describe the colors below.

- Red tastes like _____.

- Red feels like _____.

- Red looks like _____.

- Black is the color of _____.

- Black makes me feel _____.

- Black reminds me of _____.

- Blue smells like _____.

- Blue is like _____.

- Blue tastes like _____.

- Yellow _____.

- Yellow _____.

- Yellow _____.

- Green _____.

- Green _____.

- Green _____.

Replacing Common Verbs

Rewrite each sentence below, replacing each underlined word with a not-so-common verb.

1. The children <u>walked</u> to the park.

   _____

2. She <u>told</u> me that I could come to her house.

   _____

3. The hungry boy <u>ate</u> his dinner quickly.

   _____

4. The boys <u>played</u> on the field.

   _____

5. The caterpillar <u>moved</u> across the leaf.

   _____

6. Tammy <u>smiled</u> at her mother.

   _____

7. He <u>ran</u> a lap around the track.

   _____

8. The cat <u>rested</u> on the pillow.

   _____

9. She <u>slept</u> for hours.

   _____

10. I <u>held</u> the baby.

    _____

Describe a Person

Think of a person you want to describe. Write that person's name below.

_____

1. What color hair does the person have? _____

2. What color eyes does he/she have? _____

3. What does the person like to do?

   _____

4. How does the person treat you?

   _____

5. What are three words that best describe the person?

   _____   _____   _____

6. How do you feel about this person?

   _____

Write a paragraph describing this person.

_____

_____

_____

_____

_____

_____

Strong Verb Cards

ate	nibbled
gobbled	devoured
said	roared
sighed	yelled

Strong Verb Cards

looked	whispered
strolled	tiptoed
paced	stomped
walked	roared

Dramatizing Verbs Cards

He walked slowly.

She laughed loudly.

The boy was sadly looking out the window.

The girls smiled happily.

The dog barked angrily.

The lady played the piano softly.

The man turned the pages quickly.

The student read silently.

The runners ran fast.

The mother stirred slowly.

The girls whispered quietly.

The cat meowed softly.

The horse galloped quickly.

The snake slithered slowly.

The student wrote carefully.

The boys skipped happily.

The boy yelled loudly.

The mother tiptoed quietly.

The girl walked sadly.

The bell rang loudly.

The baby played quietly.

The boy ate politely.

Using Adverbs

Circle the adverb in each sentence. On the line write *when* or *how*.

1. She danced prettily down the steps. _____

2. The flowers bloomed beautifully. _____

3. Finally, she waved good-bye. _____

4. Next, we will go to recess. _____

5. Let's play quietly. _____

6. Run quickly to the store. _____

7. Tiptoe softly out of the room. _____

8. The wind blew swiftly across the lake. _____

9. We should go now. _____

10. The lady sang nicely. _____

11. The man bowed politely. _____

12. Then we went home. _____

Expository Writing

With expository writing, the writer uses his or her impression of an event or subject by collecting data through observation and/or research. The writer's goal is to increase the reader's knowledge about a certain subject or procedure by providing accurate information.

This domain often appears in the following types of writing:

- directions
- definitions
- recipes
- book reports
- memos

- commercials
- announcements
- greetings
- postcards
- invitations

- thank-you notes
- news
- summaries
- lists

Use the following activities to encourage expository writing with your children.

Research a Topic

Ask the children to identify interesting facts about your topic and write these facts on sheets of construction paper (to resemble large note cards). Arrange the facts in a logical sequence and use them to write a short research paper. (See pages 172 to 176.)

Writing Directions

Write directions for how to accomplish a task, such as tying shoes, making a sandwich, or playing a sport. Encourage the children to think carefully about all of the steps and materials needed to complete the task.

Thank You!

Saying thank you is always polite when someone volunteers time to the class. Write individual or class thank-you notes to classroom helpers, custodians, guest speakers, etc.
(See page 200.)

Concept Summaries

Write about a new concept learned in math or science. Each child writes his or her understanding of the concept. Allow the students to share their summaries with the class.
(See page 201.)

Thank You!

Write a thank-you card to a special person. Fold the paper on the dotted line to make a card.

Dear _____,

Thank you for _____

_____

It was nice of you to _____

- -

I also want to say_____

_____

Thank you again!

Sincerely,

_____

Concept Summaries

- Today I learned about _____

- The three most important things I learned were

   _____

   _____

   _____

- What I learned is interesting because

   _____

   _____

   _____

- This information is important because

   _____

   _____

   _____

- I still have questions about

   _____

   _____

   _____

Persuasive and Narrative Writing

Persuasive writing requires the writer to present facts and research in a manner that is designed to change how the reader thinks or feels about a certain subject. The writer uses anecdotes, examples, logic, or emotion to get his or her point of view across to the reader. The writer writes about a series of pictures or events, summarizes a story, collects and categorizes information into a paragraph.

This domain often includes the writing of the following:

- editorials
- letters
- advertisements
- slogans
- commercials
- speeches

Set the scene for persuasive writing by reading a story or discussing a controversial topic, such as "Should children go to school on weekends?" Have the children brainstorm ideas that might persuade others that their position is a good one. Guide the children in writing their persuasive pieces, encouraging them to use supporting sentences to back up their opinions. See page 203 for a list of persuasive writing prompts to inspire your students.

Narrative Writing

Narrative writing uses the imagination and storytelling skills to retell an event that is either real or imaginary. The writer uses his or her own words and imagination to tell a story or retell an event. The writer creates imaginary people, animals, and/or events. He or she writes original stories on a topic.

This domain includes the writing of the following:

- anecdotes
- short stories
- poetry
- folktales
- myths

See page 205 for a list of narrative writing prompts.

Persuasive Writing Prompts

Use the following prompts to inspire persuasive writing:

- ❖ Is it important to have school rules?
- ❖ Should children have to eat vegetables?
- ❖ Was Goldilocks a good girl?
- ❖ Is it important to keep your desk clean?
- ❖ Is it important to keep your room clean?
- ❖ Is it important to brush your teeth every day?
- ❖ Should people have to take turns?
- ❖ Is it okay to lie?
- ❖ Should brothers and sisters have to share toys?
- ❖ Should parents be in charge?
- ❖ Is it important to help others?
- ❖ Which shape is better—a circle or a square?
- ❖ Should children be allowed to vote for president?
- ❖ Is it okay to litter?
- ❖ Is recess a good idea?
- ❖ Is it important to learn the letters of the alphabet?
- ❖ If you found 10 dollars on the floor in a store, would it be okay to keep the money?
- ❖ Is it safe to ride a bike or inline skates without a helmet?
- ❖ Write an ad for your favorite cereal. Why should people buy one brand of cereal instead of another?
- ❖ Is the Big Bad Wolf really bad or just misunderstood?

Duplicate page 204 for each student to use for addressing one of these controversial issues.

Controversial Issues

Question (Write the controversial question here.)

_____

- What is your opinion?

_____

_____

_____

- What are your reasons for this opinion?

_____

_____

_____

_____

- Why might someone feel differently about this issue?

_____

_____

_____

_____

Write a paragraph expressing your opinion and reasons altogether.

_____

_____

_____

_____

_____

_____

_____

Narrative Writing Prompts

Use the following prompts to inspire narrative writing:

- ❖ On the first day of school, I was/felt . . .
- ❖ The best day of my life was when . . .
- ❖ My most embarrassing moment was when . . .
- ❖ The worst day of my life was . . .
- ❖ When I grow up, I want to be . . .
- ❖ My favorite place to visit is . . .
- ❖ If I were the president, I would . . .
- ❖ Retell a favorite fairy tale.
- ❖ Write about a hobby.
- ❖ My favorite thing about school is . . .
- ❖ Pretend you are a dinosaur. What is your life like?
- ❖ Tell about a field trip your class took.
- ❖ Tell about a time that you made a new friend.
- ❖ Write about something funny that happened to you.
- ❖ Describe a favorite holiday.
- ❖ Have you ever slept at a friend's house or had a friend sleep at your house? What did you and your friend do?
- ❖ Tell about a time you got in trouble. What did you do?
- ❖ Describe what happened when you got stuck in the rain.
- ❖ How do you spend your time on the weekends?
- ❖ What was it like learning to tie your shoes by yourself?
- ❖ What is it like to eat in the cafeteria?
- ❖ What games do you like to play at recess?
- ❖ Tell about riding on the school bus.
- ❖ How does it feel to ride a bike?
- ❖ Tell about a time you skinned your knee.
- ❖ Tell about a visit to the dentist or doctor.
- ❖ Tell about something that was once hard for you to do, but is now easy for you to do.

Checking for Spelling

Mini-Dictionary

Learning to use the dictionary is a difficult but necessary skill for young children. Help the students understand the need for dictionaries by providing them with their own mini-dictionaries filled with high-frequency words.

Materials

- copies of pages 207–213 for each student
- scissors
- stapler
- pencils

1. Distribute pages 207–213 to each student.

2. Assist the students in cutting apart the pages and assembling them into booklets.

3. Review the high-frequency words on each page. Explain that a booklet filled with these words can be helpful when writing.

4. Draw students' attention to the blanks on each page and explain that these lines are provided for them to add new words that are meaningful to them.

5. Encourage the students to refer to their personal dictionaries often.

ABC Order

In order for students to effectively use dictionaries, they need to have a solid understanding of alphabetical order. A child could spend hours looking for a word in the dictionary without knowledge of how the words are sequenced.

1. Distribute pages 214 and 215 to provide practice for students with understanding alphabetical order.

2. You will also find pages that feature the skill of identifying letters that are found at the beginning, the middle, and the end of the dictionary.

3. This skill helps to simplify dictionary use even more.

Mini-Dictionary

_____'s

Dictionary

A

about _____

after _____

again _____

always _____

and _____

_____

_____

_____

B

because _____

been _____

before _____

both _____

bring _____

buy _____

by _____

_____

_____

C

came _____

carry _____

come _____

could _____

_____

_____

_____

_____

Mini-Dictionary *(cont.)*

D

does   _____

don't   _____

done   _____

down   _____

_____   _____

_____   _____

_____   _____

_____   _____

E

eat   _____

eight   _____

ever   _____

every   _____

everything   _____

_____   _____

_____   _____

F

find   _____

for   _____

found   _____

four   _____

friend   _____

funny   _____

_____   _____

_____   _____

_____   _____

G

goes   _____

going   _____

good   _____

got   _____

_____   _____

_____   _____

_____   _____

_____   _____

Mini-Dictionary (cont.)

H

have _____

help _____

here _____

hurt _____

_____ _____

_____ _____

_____ _____

_____ _____

I

into _____

is _____

it _____

_____ _____

_____ _____

_____ _____

_____ _____

J

jump _____

just _____

_____ _____

_____ _____

_____ _____

_____ _____

_____ _____

K

keep _____

kind _____

know _____

_____ _____

_____ _____

_____ _____

_____ _____

Mini-Dictionary *(cont.)*

L

laugh _____

let _____

light _____

like _____

little _____

live _____

look _____

_____ _____

_____ _____

_____ _____

M

made _____

make _____

many _____

most _____

much _____

myself _____

_____ _____

_____ _____

_____ _____

N

never _____

new _____

nothing _____

now _____

_____ _____

_____ _____

_____ _____

_____ _____

O

off _____

once _____

one _____

over _____

own _____

_____ _____

_____ _____

_____ _____

_____ _____

Mini-Dictionary *(cont.)*

P

play _____

please _____

pretty _____

put _____

_____ _____

_____ _____

_____ _____

_____ _____

Q

question _____

quiet _____

_____ _____

_____ _____

_____ _____

_____ _____

_____ _____

_____ _____

R

read _____

ride _____

right _____

_____ _____

_____ _____

_____ _____

_____ _____

_____ _____

S

said _____

saw _____

say _____

sleep _____

some _____

soon _____

_____ _____

_____ _____

_____ _____

Mini-Dictionary *(cont.)*

T

thank

the

them

there

their

today

together

U

under

upon

us

use

V

very

W

walk

want

wear

were

where

which

Mini-Dictionary *(cont.)*

X

x-ray

Y

yellow

yes

you

yours

Z

zero

Notes

Where Is It?

When looking for a word in a dictionary, it is helpful to know if it will be found at the beginning, middle, or end. Read and cut out each word below. Where will the word be found in the dictionary? Glue the word onto the correct tree trunk.

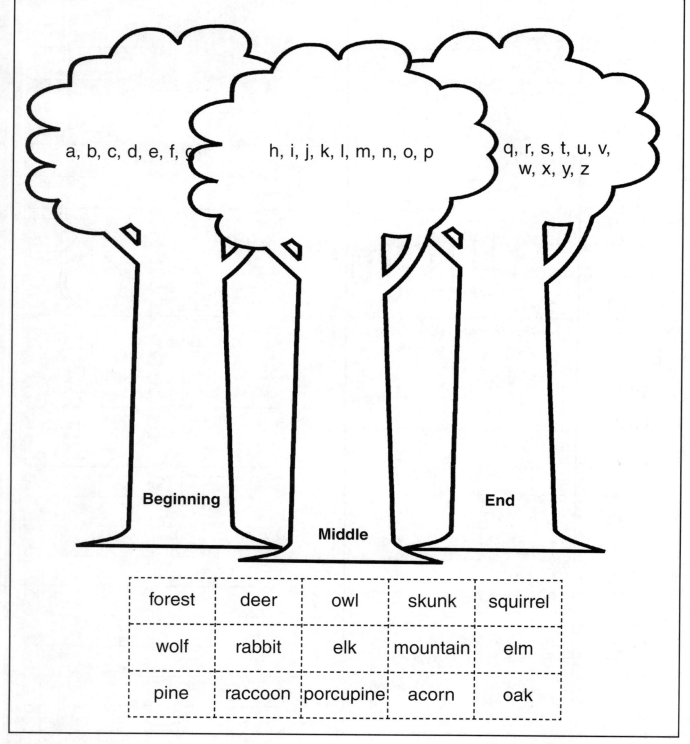

a, b, c, d, e, f, g   h, i, j, k, l, m, n, o, p   q, r, s, t, u, v, w, x, y, z

Beginning   **Middle**   **End**

forest	deer	owl	skunk	squirrel
wolf	rabbit	elk	mountain	elm
pine	raccoon	porcupine	acorn	oak

Order in the Pet Store!

Understanding alphabetical order makes dictionary use much easier! Put each group of words in ABC order.

puppy _____

pet _____

plenty _____

kitten _____

kitchen_____

kite _____

bird _____

basket _____

boy _____

lizard _____

love _____

lots _____

frog _____

fun _____

fast _____

mouse _____

mud _____

milk _____

Assessment

Perhaps one of the most difficult elements of language arts instruction is the area of assessment. Most teachers struggle with how to effectively evaluate their students' progress and communicate this progress to parents.

It is important to remember that teaching and assessing are inseparable processes. Assessment, which is typically viewed as evaluating what a child is doing wrong, should instead be about identifying what a child is able to do and what he or she is ready to learn next.

There are many types of assessment that can be helpful when evaluating progress in writing development. You, as the professional, will be able to determine which method serves your program best.

Authentic Assessment

Authentic assessment is the evaluation of tasks that bear resemblance to reading and writing in the real world. The goal is to assess literacy abilities in context. This involves the reading of real texts and writing about meaningful topics. Such tasks can include the discussion of books, writing in journals, and writing and revising original written pieces. The focus is not only on the finished product, but, more importantly, on the process and thinking behind the work.

Authentic assessment tasks are learning experiences in themselves and do not involve recall of information or the isolation of individual skills, but rather encourage students to apply their knowledge to certain tasks.

Assessment can be formal or informal. Formal assessments typically provide teachers with a "systematic way to evaluate how well students are progressing in a particular instructional program." For example, after teaching a unit of study, the teacher evaluates how well the children understand important skills and concepts through the use of real reading and writing tasks that are suitable for the instruction that has taken place. It is important to remember that with authentic assessment, the evaluation is ongoing and integrated with classroom instruction. The goal is to assess the future direction of learning and instruction, rather than to assign a grade.

Formal Assessment

Formal assessment sometimes takes on the form of standardized testing. School districts and states often depend on these to gather information about how children are doing in comparison to other children at the same grade level.

Informal Assessment

Informal assessment involves the use of very different kinds of evaluation tasks. The focus might be on a group task, individual projects, participation in experiments, class assignments, journal entries, or group discussions. Informal assessment can also involve the use of teacher checklists, anecdotal records, or informal conferencing.

Using a wide variety of assessment tools assists you, as the professional, in gaining an understanding of each child's progress and goals for future instructional activities.

Portfolio Assessment

Many assessment instruments tend to be too narrow in focus and don't reflect children's true abilities. Portfolio assessment is often considered a more desirable method of evaluating students' writing because it does not reduce the child to an impersonalized number or letter grade.

Because writing is a process, using a portfolio is the best way to show student progress. Portfolios also allow students a means to demonstrate their understanding of each step in the writing process. A portfolio can be made with a three-ring folder or binder or in an expanding folder. There should be a portfolio for each student. Write the name of the student on the outside of the folder so it can be easily located (see page 218). Keep the portfolios in a basket or box on a counter or in a lower file cabinet drawer so you and your students can access them easily. Keep samples of student work throughout the year. Be sure not to make the portfolio a huge collection of writings, but rather a place to hold specific pieces that are organized by learning goals.

Encourage your children to select work samples for their portfolios that represent things they have learned. For example, a child may be proud of the fact that he or she has perfected the use of punctuation or the spellings of certain words. This child might select a piece to reflect this progress. You should also have the children label each piece of work in the portfolio, telling why it was selected and how this piece shows progress (see page 219).

Portfolios can include more than just writing samples. You might also want to include the following items:

- anecdotal observations (comments or samples of oral language)
- audiotapes (of stories read or other oral language events)
- video tapes
- notes from individual conferences
- literacy attitude surveys
- teacher checklists
- self-assessment checklists
- rubrics

Duplicate the tips on page 220 to assist you in the use of portfolios.

Checklists

Checklists provide concise outlines for teachers. They serve the evaluative process best if used periodically throughout the year.

Page 221 provides a checklist that you can duplicate to use in your classroom.

Rubrics

Rubrics are helpful in writing evaluation because they provide the teacher with a set of criteria and standards by which to score. You can design your own rubrics for particular assignments or use rubrics that have already been created for your use (see pages 222 and 223).

My Portfolio

Name _____

Portfolio Description Slips

Teacher Note: Have students complete the slips below. Attach them to students' work before placing in their portfolios.

I chose this for my portfolio because

_____

_____

I chose this for my portfolio because

_____

_____

I chose this for my portfolio because

_____

_____

I am proud of this because

_____

_____

I am proud of this because

_____

_____

I am proud of this because

_____

_____

Teacher's Guide

Portfolios *(cont.)*

Keep the following points in mind when using portfolios:

1. The portfolio belongs to the student. Encourage students to take pride in their work. Be careful of the notes and comments that you make on student work. Be sure that the comments are dignified and encouraging. Nobody wants to save and repeatedly look at an assignment with negative comments on it.

2. Add samples regularly, but not too often. Too many papers and samples can be overwhelming to organize.

3. Add a variety of samples documenting various phases of the writing process. Selecting the best example of each stage in the process may give a better picture of what the student is able to do, but including beginning samples of a stage as well as more developed samples can show progress.

4. Review portfolios frequently. Be sure to include times to look through the portfolios. Giving students suggestions on what to look for as they review their portfolios is an effective way to use the portfolio. Don't just ask students to look through their portfolios. Point out progress and insights to their writing process. Be their guide as they learn about themselves as writers.

5. Note the progress of each student. Be sure to set up times to meet individually with each student. Acknowledge and praise progress. Discuss suggestions for each student to improve his or her writing. Be concise. Don't give too many suggestions, as your message may get lost.

6. Share with parents. Allow parents to review the portfolio. You may wish to have a homework assignment for students to review their portfolios with parents. Encourage parents to write positive comments about their child's writing and progress.

7. Allow time for students to write or dictate a reflection about their writing and their writing abilities. These reflections will show progression and growth as well.

Teacher's Guide

Teacher Checklist for Report Writing Standards

Skill	First Attempt	Mastery
1. Demonstrates competence in the general skills and strategies of the writing process.		
Prewriting		
A. Uses prewriting strategies to plan written work.		
discusses ideas with peers		
draws pictures to generate ideas		
writes key thoughts and questions		
rehearses ideas		
records reactions and observations		
Drafting and Revising		
B. Uses strategies to draft and revise written work.		
rereads		
rearranges words, sentences, and paragraphs to improve or clarify meaning		
varies sentence types		
adds descriptive words and details		
deletes extraneous information		
incorporates suggestions from peers and teachers		
sharpens the focus		
Editing and Publishing		
C. Uses strategies to edit and publish written work.		
proofreads using a dictionary and other resources		
edits for grammar, punctuation, capitalization, and spelling at appropriate developmental level		
incorporates illustrations or photos		
shares finished product		
D. Evaluates own and others' writing.		
asks questions and makes comments about writing		
helps classmates apply grammatical and mechanical conventions		
E. Dictates or writes with a logical sequence of events (includes beginning, middle, end).		
F. Dictates or writes detailed descriptions of familiar persons, places, objects, or experiences.		
G. Writes in response to literature.		
H. Writes in a variety of formats (picture books, letters, stories, poems, information pieces).		

Six-Point Rubric

❏ **Six Points: Fluent Writer**

The student is able to write a paragraph (three or more sentences) on a specific topic. The paragraph contains a main idea with supporting sentences. Common words and sight words are spelled correctly. Correct grammar and punctuation are used. Self-editing is evident. There is variety in the sentence structures which adds interest and detail to what the writer has to say.

❏ **Five Points: Confident Writer**

The student is able to write a paragraph (three or more sentences) on a specific topic. The paragraph contains a main idea with supporting sentences. Most of the common words and sight words are spelled correctly. Correct grammar and punctuation are used most of the time. The student is beginning to self-edit his or her writing.

❏ **Four Points: Capable Writer**

The student is able to write two or three sentences on a specific topic. Each sentence begins with a capital letter and ends with the appropriate punctuation. The student uses phonetic spelling for new words and is able to spell many sight words correctly.

❏ **Two Points: Beginning Writer**

The student is beginning to develop knowledge of sound-letter correspondence. One or two words are used in the "sentence." Capital letters at the beginning of the sentences and the appropriate punctuation at the end of the sentences are not used.

❏ **One Point: Pre-Writer**

The student has little knowledge of sound-letter relationships. Scribbles or random letters are used in his or her writing.

Story Writing Assessment Rubric

Use the rubric below to assess student progress of the mechanics and grammar standards.

Competent

- ❏ The student can independently demonstrate competence in the writing process.
- ❏ The student can independently use prewriting strategies to plan a story.
- ❏ The student can independently use strategies to draft a story.
- ❏ The student can independently use strategies to revise a story.
- ❏ The student can independently use strategies to edit a story.
- ❏ The student can independently use strategies to publish a written story.
- ❏ The student can independently evaluate his or her stories.
- ❏ The student can independently evaluate others' stories.
- ❏ The student can independently show competence in stylistic/rhetorical aspects of writing.
- ❏ The student can independently use general, frequently used words to convey basic ideas.

Emergent

- ❏ The student can usually demonstrate competence in the writing process.
- ❏ The student can usually use prewriting strategies to plan a story.
- ❏ The student can usually use strategies to draft a story.
- ❏ The student can usually use strategies to revise a story.
- ❏ The student can usually use strategies to edit a story.
- ❏ The student can usually use strategies to publish a written story.
- ❏ The student can usually evaluate his or her stories.
- ❏ The student can usually evaluate others' stories.
- ❏ The student can usually demonstrate competence in stylistic and rhetorical aspects of writing.
- ❏ The student can usually use general, frequently used words to convey basic ideas.

Beginner

- ❏ The student requires assistance to demonstrate competence in the writing process.
- ❏ The student requires assistance to use prewriting strategies to plan a story.
- ❏ The student requires assistance to use strategies to draft a story.
- ❏ The student requires assistance to use strategies to revise a story.
- ❏ The student requires assistance to use strategies to edit a story.
- ❏ The student requires assistance to use strategies to publish a written story.
- ❏ The student requires assistance to evaluate his or her stories.
- ❏ The student requires assistance to evaluate others' stories.
- ❏ The student requires assistance to show competence in stylistic and rhetorical aspects of writing.
- ❏ The student requires assistance to use general, frequently used words to convey basic ideas.

Assessment Notes

_____   _____

_____   _____

_____   _____

_____   _____

_____   _____

_____   _____

_____   _____

_____   _____

_____   _____

_____   _____

_____   _____

_____   _____

_____   _____

_____   _____

Part II

Writer's Notebook

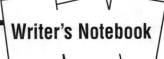

Writing Process Checklist

Use this checklist to keep track of your work in the writing process.

❏ **Prewriting**

Generate ideas for writing (brainstorm, create a story map, make a word bank, etc.).

Date: _____ _____ _____ _____ _____ _____

❏ **Rough Draft**

Write your ideas on paper.

Date: _____ _____ _____ _____ _____ _____

❏ **Reread**

Read your story out loud to make sure you have written clearly.

Date: _____ _____ _____ _____ _____ _____

❏ **Share with a Friend**

Share your written work with a classmate.

Date: _____ _____ _____ _____ _____ _____

❏ **Revise**

Improve your writing by adding details, interesting language, and suggestions from your classmate.

Date: _____ _____ _____ _____ _____ _____

❏ **Editing**

Work with a friend to correct errors in spelling and punctuation.

Date: _____ _____ _____ _____ _____ _____

❏ **Final Draft**

Write your final copy of the story.

Date: _____ _____ _____ _____ _____ _____

❏ **Publishing**

Publish your story by making a book, placing your story on display, or reading it aloud to the class.

Date: _____ _____ _____ _____ _____ _____

Brainstorming Topics

Write your story ideas below.

- Dreams

- School Events

- Family Members

- Animals

- Hobbies

- Things I Like

- Things I Don't Like

My Memoirs

Are you ready for the task of writing about your life? Use this page to write your ideas for stories to tell about your life.

- Family Stories

  _____   _____

  _____   _____

- Vacation Stories

  _____   _____

  _____   _____

- Pet Stories

  _____   _____

  _____   _____

- Earliest Memories

  _____   _____

  _____   _____

- Grandparents

  _____   _____

  _____   _____

- Best Friends

  _____   _____

  _____   _____

- Funny Stories

  _____   _____

  _____   _____

- Sad Stories

  _____   _____

  _____   _____

- Scary Stories

  _____   _____

  _____   _____

"Said" Words

- agreed

- answered

- begged

- cried

- cried out

- demanded

- exclaimed

- giggled

- groaned

- insisted

- _____

- _____

- _____

- joked

- laughed

- lied

- mumbled

- replied

- responded

- roared

- screamed

- sobbed

- yelled

- _____

- _____

- _____

Self-Assessment Checklist

Take a good look at your writing. Use this checklist to help you make your final corrections.

	Yes	No
Does my writing look nice and neat?		
Is my writing clear? Does it make sense?		
Did I have a friend read it?		
Did he or she suggest changes?		
Did I indent each paragraph?		
Did I check for proper spelling?		
Did I check for proper capitalization and punctuation?		

Here is what I think of my writing:

_____

_____

Synonyms

- **bad**—awful, terrible, unpleasant

- **big**—large, huge, gigantic, enormous

- **close**—shut, slam

- **fast**—speedy, rapid, quick

- **give**—offer, donate

- **good**—fine, excellent, delightful

- **help**—assist, aid, lend a hand

- **know**—understand, recognize

- **let**—allow, permit

- **like**—enjoy, fond of

- **long**—lengthy, stretched out

- _____

- _____

- **new**—fresh, original

- **old**—elderly, ancient

- **play**—frolic, romp, have fun

- **small**—tiny, petite, little

- **say**—reply, respond, answer

- **tell**—inform, declare, advise

- **very**—extremely, especially, incredibly

- **weird**—odd, bizarre, creepy

- _____

- _____

- _____

- _____

Homophones

ant (insect)	**aunt** (parent's sister)	
ate (as food)	**eight** (number)	
buy (purchase)	**by** (beside)	**bye** (as goodbye)
cent (penny)	**sent** (mailed)	**scent** (odor)
dear (darling)	**deer** (animal)	
flew (in air)	**flu** (illness)	
for	**four** (number)	
hear (listen)	**here** (now)	
hole (tear or gap)	**whole** (all)	
hour (sixty minutes)	**our** (belonging to us)	
knew	**new** (not used)	
knot (in a rope)	**not**	
meat (food)	**meet**	
one (number)	**won**	
right (correct)	**write**	
road (street)	**rode**	
sea (ocean)	**see** (look)	
tail	**tale** (story)	
their (belonging to them)	**there**	**they're** (they are)
to	**too** (also)	**two** (number)
weak (not strong)	**week** (seven days)	
wood (from a tree)	**would**	

Similes

- blind as a bat

- brave as a lion

- clean as a whistle

- cold as ice

- easy as pie

- free as the breeze

- good as gold

- green as grass

- hard as nails

- light as a feather

- playful as a kitten

- pretty as a picture

- proud as a peacock

- sharp as a tack

- sly as a fox

- smart as a whip

- straight as an arrow

- strong as an ox

- stubborn as a mule

- white as a sheet

- wrinkled as a prune

- _____

- _____

- _____

- _____

- _____

Idioms

Idiom	Figurative Meaning
spill the beans	tell a secret
hold your horses	be patient
hit the ceiling	get mad
hold your tongue	stay quiet
in a pickle	having a problem
in one ear and out the other	don't pay attention
raining cats and dogs	raining very hard
cat got your tongue	don't know what to say
feeling under the weather	not feeling well
got up on the wrong side of the bed	in a bad mood

Onomatopoeia

- bam
- bang
- boing
- buzz
- chomp
- choo
- chugga chugga
- crunch
- crash
- grrr
- purr
- roar
- screech
- smack
- splat

- ugh
- vroom
- eek
- squeek
- squawk
- whoo whoo
- crackle
- woof
- meow
- aah
- aachoo
- ssh
- tweet
- snap
- fizz

Now write a few of your own.

- _____
- _____
- _____

- _____
- _____
- _____

Friendly Letter Template

_____
Date

Dear _____,
greeting

_____

_____

_____

_____

_____

_____

_____

_____

_____,
closing

_____
signature

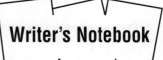

Business Letter Template

_____

sender's street address

_____

sender's city, state, and zip code

_____

date

_____

recipient's name

_____

recipient's street address

_____

recipient's city, state, and zip code

Dear _____:

greeting

_____

_____

_____

_____

_____

_____

_____,

closing

_____

signature

Friendly Letter Greetings

• Dear _____,

• Hi _____,

• Hello _____,

• Dearest _____,

Business Letter Greetings

• Dear Sir:

• Dear Madam:

• Dear Sir or Madam:

• To Whom It May Concern:

Friendly Letter Closings

• Yours truly,   • Regards,

• Love,   • Best wishes,

• Your friend,   • With love,

• Fondly,

Business Letter Closings

• Sincerely,

• Respectfully yours,

• Sincerely yours,

Addressing an Envelope

Sender's name

Street address

City, State, Zip Code

Recipient's name

Street address

City, State, Zip Code

Addressing an Envelope: State Abbreviations

Alabama—AL

Alaska—AK

Arizona—AZ

Arkansas—AR

California—CA

Colorado—CO

Connecticut—CT

Delaware—DE

Florida—FL

Georgia—GA

Hawaii—HI

Idaho—ID

Illinois—IL

Indiana—IN

Iowa—IA

Kansas—KA

Kentucky—KY

Louisiana—LA

Maine—ME

Maryland—MD

Massachusetts—MA

Michigan—MI

Minnesota—MN

Mississippi—MS

Missouri—MO

Montana—MT

Nebraska—NE

Nevada—NV

New Hampshire—NH

New Jersey—NJ

New Mexico—NM

New York—NY

North Carolina—NC

North Dakota—ND

Ohio—OH

Oklahoma—OK

Oregon—OR

Pennsylvania—PA

Rhode Island—RI

South Carolina—SC

South Dakota—SD

Tennessee—TN

Texas—TX

Utah—UT

Vermont—VT

Virginia—VA

Washington—WA

West Virginia—WV

Wisconsin—WI

Wyoming—WY

Writing a News Article

_____

Headline

Author: _____ Date: _____

What happened? _____

_____

_____

_____

Where did it happen?

_____

_____

Who was involved?

_____

_____

Why did it happen?

_____

_____

How did it happen?

_____

_____

_____

_____

_____

Writing a Book Report

Include the following elements in your book report.

Book title _____

Author _____

Main character(s) _____

_____

Setting _____

_____

Main Idea of the Story

_____

_____

_____

_____

_____

_____

_____

_____

My Recommendation

_____

_____

_____

_____

_____

Proofreading Symbols

Symbol	Meaning	Example
∧	insert	o it
و	Omit or take out	exercise ran often
≡	capitalize	mary
/	use a lowercase letter	The President sat down.
⌐	remove all caps	Do you SEE what I mean?
⌒	join words together	chalk board
¶	new paragraph	for the day. Some people
⊙	add a period	The dog ran fast⊙
⌒	add a comma	However that is not always true.
#	add a space	today. If thats how

Writing a Cinquain Poem

Line 1:   Noun

Line 2:   Two adjectives

Line 3:   Three verbs

Line 4:   Four-word phrase or sentence

Line 5:   Renaming noun

Cinquain Outline

_____

_____   _____

_____   _____   _____

_____

_____

Writing a Color Poem

❏ _____ is _____.

❏ _____ is _____.

❏ _____ is _____.

❏ _____ is _____.

❏ _____ tastes like _____.

❏ _____ smells like _____.

❏ _____ sounds like _____.

❏ _____ feels like _____.

❏ _____ looks like _____.

❏ _____ makes me _____.

❏ _____ is _____.

Writing Shape Poems

Heart

Spiral

Ice-cream cone

Sun

Writing a Haiku Poem

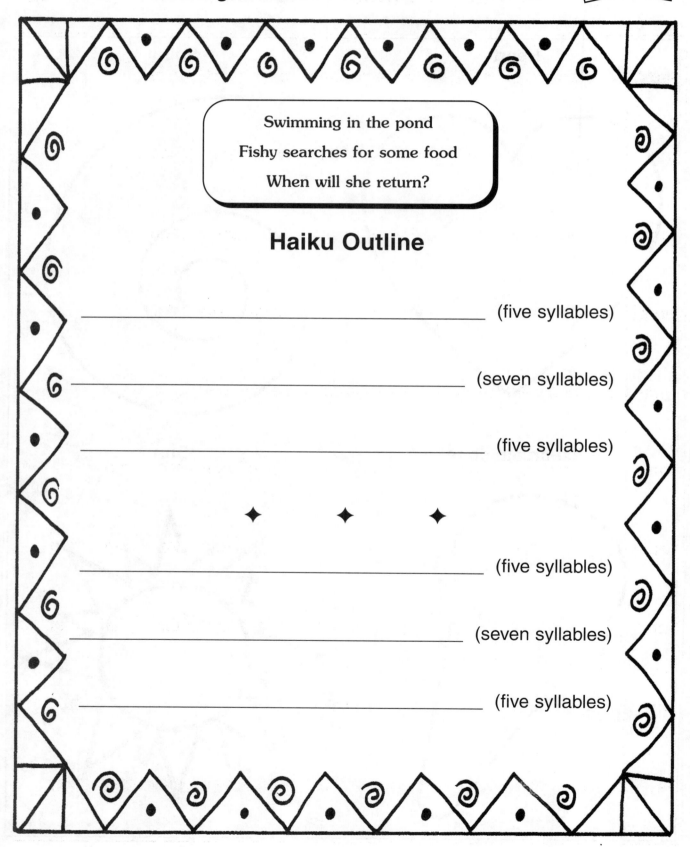

Swimming in the pond
Fishy searches for some food
When will she return?

Haiku Outline

_____ (five syllables)

_____ (seven syllables)

_____ (five syllables)

◆   ◆   ◆

_____ (five syllables)

_____ (seven syllables)

_____ (five syllables)

Word Families

-ack	back pack tack snack rack black sack crack quack
-ail	bail nail sail trail pail tail mail rail snail
-ain	rain drain stain main vain grain train pain brain
-ake	bake lake take shake cake make wake snake fake
-ame	came game same flame frame name blame
-an	ban man tan plan can pan van scan fan ran
-ap	cap map sap clap gap nap tap snap lap rap trap
-at	fat rat flat bat mat sat scat cat pat chat that
-ate	gate rate plate date late skate state
-ay	bay hay pay way day lay ray clay may say play

Word Families *(cont.)*

-eat	heat seat beat meat neat cheat treat
-ell	bell fell well spell sell shell tell smell
-est	best nest west test vest
-ice	mice price twice dice nice slice rice spice
-ick	sick brick kick pick tick chick lick quick wick trick
-ide	side bride slide hide tide glide ride wide pride inside
-ight	fight night tight fright light right bright might sight flight
-ill	fill pill drill bill hill will grill chill skill
-in	tin grin pin win skin fin chin thin
-ine	dine mine fine pine line vine spine

Word Families *(cont.)*

-oat	boat	coat	goat					
-oast	boast	coast	roast	toast				
-oke	joke	poke	woke	broke	smoke			
-one	bone	cone	phone	stone	tone	zone		
-op	cop	drop	mop	pop	top	stop		
-ot	got	hot	lot	not	pot	rot	tot	slot	trot
-ut	but	cut	gut	hut	nut	rut	strut	shut	
-um	bum	chum	gum	hum	drum			
-ug	bug	chug	dug	hug	jug	mug	rug	slug	tug
-un	bun	fun	run	sun	stun			

Adjectives

Size Words	Shape Words	Personality Words
bulky	crooked	bold
immense	curved	ferocious
massive	long	gentle
towering	shallow	kind
	square	shy
	wide	vicious

Color Words	Texture Words	Weather Words
bright	cold	breezy
glowing	damp	dusty
dull	gooey	foggy
pale	oily	frosty
dazzling	rough	hazy
radiant	slimy	humid
shiny	slippery	stormy
	sticky	windy

Synonyms for Emotions

Happy	Sad	Angry
glad	disappointed	annoyed
cheerful	discouraged	irritated
thrilled	lonely	fuming
proud	gloomy	irate
joyful	tearful	livid
content	troubled	furious
delighted	anxious	
ecstatic		

Story Structure

Beginning

❏ Present main characters.

❏ Describe the setting.

❏ Introduce the problem.

Middle

❏ Give more information about the problem.

❏ How does the character try to solve the problem?

End

❏ Describe the most exciting part of the story.

❏ Describe how the problem is solved.

Character Description

- ❏   What is the character's name?

- ❏   What does the character look like?

- ❏   How old is the character?

- ❏   What color hair does the character have?

- ❏   What is the character's personality like?

- ❏   What talents does the character have?

- ❏   What problem does the character have?

Answer Key

Page 50

Answers may vary.

1. Is it a nice spring day?
2. Was that your brother in the lunch room?
3. When is it time to plant the garden?
4. Do you love playing soccer?
5. What is your favorite book?
6. Did you take your time on the spelling test?
7. Who is that man?
8. Did you have fun at the baseball game?

Page 51

Answers will vary.

Page 85

Accept appropriate answers.

Page 100

1. would
2. about
3. friend
4. have
5. goes
6. what, they
7. What, come
8. laugh
9. eight
10. what

Page 101

1. question mark
2. question mark
3. period
4. period
5. question mark
6. exclamation mark
7. exclamation mark
8. period

Page 102

1. It's time for school.
2. When is your birthday?
3. Tony is on the playground.
4. Did you see the thunderstorm?
5. Summer is my favorite time of year.
6. Let me help you with that.
7. Kelly, what are you doing?
8. I can't wait for vacation.

Page 103

1. What are you doing after the game?
2. Thank you for helping me.
3. Did you know that I'm on the team?
4. I have too many hamsters.
5. How many pets does she have?
6. She helped me because she's nice.
7. Let's go to the game together.
8. Where do you live?

Page 145

1. I'll be watching you.
2. Be quiet.
3. S
4. M
5. S
6. S
7. M
8. ribbit or croak
9. slam, bang, etc.
10. whoo, whoo
11. A
12. A
13. P
14. P

Page 162

1. AK
2. WY
3. NC
4. OK
5. CO
6. NM
7. WA
8. IN
9. DE
10. NV
11. CA
12. OH
13. AZ
14. MT

Page 163

James Chang
2275 South Hudson
Denver, CO 80234

Mike Jesson
19847 Court Street
Chino Hills, CA 91709

Jody Heinrich
13221 Rolling Hills Lane
Dallas, TX 75240

Amy Settle
854 Higby Road
Utica, NY 13035

Randy Hoffner
8843 North Forest Lane
Flagstaff, AZ 86004

Shirley Chen
12875 East Valley Road
Chandler AZ 85224

Pam Wilburn
843 South Street
Redmond, WA 98052

Page 198

1. prettily (how)
2. beautifully (how)
3. Finally (when)
4. Next (when)
5. quietly (how)
6. quickly (how)
7. softly (how)
8. swiftly (how)
9. now (when)
10. nicely (how)
11. politely (how)
12. then (when)

Page 214

Beginning: forest, deer, elk, acorn, elm

Middle: pine, owl, porcupine, mountain, oak

End: wolf, rabbit, raccoon, skunk, squirrel

Page 215

pet, plenty, puppy

kitchen, kite, kitten

basket, bird, boy

lizard, lots, love

fast, ferret, friend

hamster, hat, home

References

Fiction

Aliki. *Tabby: A Story in Pictures.* HarperCollins, 1995.

Allard, Harry and Marshall, James. *Miss Nelson Is Back.* Houghton Mifflin, 1988.

Anno, Mitsumasa. *Anno's Counting Book.* Crowell, 1977.

Baker, Jeanne. *Home.* Greenwillow, 2004.

Window. Greenwillow, 1991.

Barrett, Judi. *Cloudy with a Chance of Meatballs.* Aladdin, 1982.

Base, Graeme. *Animalia.* Harry N. Abrams, 1987.

The Sign of the Seahorse. Puffin, 1998.

Baylor, Byrd. *I'm in Charge of Celebrations.* Aladdin, 1995.

Briggs, Raymond. *The Snowman.* Random House, 1986.

Calmenson, Stephanie. *The Principal's New Clothes.* Scholastic, 1991.

Day, Alexandra. *Follow Carl!* Farrar, Straus & Giroux, 1998.

Good Dog, Carl. Demco Media, 1997.

dePaola, Tomie. *Do You Want to Be My Friend?* Putnam, 1988.

The Legend of the Bluebonnet. Puffin, 1996.

Pancakes for Breakfast. Voyager Books, 1978.

Fox, Mem. *Possum Magic.* Voyager Books, 1991.

Time for Bed. Gulliver Books, 1993.

Wilfrid Gordon McDonald Partridge. Scott Foresman, 1989.

Greenberg, David. *Slugs.* Megan Tingley, 1983.

Heller, Ruth. *Many Luscious Lollipops.* Puffin, 1998.

Hutchins, Pat. *Changes, Changes.* Macmillan, 1971.

Rosie's Walk. Turtleback, 1971.

Joyce, William. *George Shrinks.* Laura Geringer, 1985.

Keats, Ezra Jack. *Clementina's Cactus.* Viking Children's Books, 1999.

Lobel, Arnold. *Fables.* HarperCollins, 1980.

McCully, Emily Arnold. *Four Hungry Kittens.* Dial Books, 2001.

Mayer, Mercer. *One Frog Too Many.* Dial Books, 2003.

There's a Nightmare in My Closet. Puffin, 1992.

Munsch, Robert. *The Paper Bag Princess.* Annick Press, 1992.

Polacco, Patricia. *Mrs. Katz and Tush.* Yearling Books, 1994.

Pink and Say. Philomel Books, 1994.

Raschka, Chris. *Yo! Yes?* Orchard Books, 1998.

Ringgold, Faith. *Tar Beach.* Dragonfly, 1996.

Rylant, Cynthia. *When I Was Young in the Mountains.* Puffin, 1993.

The Relatives Came. Pearson Learning, 1993.

San Souci, Robert. *The Talking Eggs: a Folktale from the American South.* Schlastic, 1994.

Scieszka, Jon. *The True Story of the Three Little Pigs.* Puffin, 1997.

References

Sendak, Maurice. *Where the Wild Things Are.* HarperCollins, 1988.

Sharmat, Marjorie Weinman. *Gila Monsters Meet You at the Airport.* Scott Foresman, 1990.

Sharmat, Mitchell. *Gregory, the Terrible Eater.* Scholastic, 1989.

Sis, Peter. *Dinosaur.* Greenwillow, 2000.

    An Ocean World. HarperCollins, 1992.

Spier, Peter. *Peter Spier's Rain.* Bt Binding, 1999.

Thaler, Mike. *The Teacher from the Black Lagoon.* Scholastic, 1989.

Van Allsburg, Chris. *Jumanji.* Houghton Mifflin, 1981.

    Mysteries of Harris Burdick. Houghton Mifflin, 1984.

    The Wreck of the Zephyr. Houghton Mifflin, 1983.

    Two Bad Ants. Houghton Mifflin, 1988.

Viorst, Judith. *Alexander, and the Terrible, Horrible, No Good, Very Bad Day.* Aladdin, 1987.

    Alexander, Who Used to be Rich Last Sunday. Scott Foresman, 1987.

    If I Were in Charge of the World and Other Worries. Scott Foresman, 1984.

    I'll Fix Anthony. Aladdin, 1988.

White, E.B. *Charlotte's Web.* HarperTrophy, 1974.

Wiesner, David. *Free Fall.* HarperTrophy, 1991.

    Tuesday. Clarion, 1991.

    Sector 7. Houghton Mifflin, 1999.

Wilder, Laura Ingalls. *Little House in the Big Woods.* HarperTrophy, 1953.

Williams, Vera B. *A Chair for My Mother.* Greenwillow, 1982.

    Stringbean's Trip to the Shining Sea. HarperTrophy, 1999.

Wing, Natasha. *The Night Before Kindergarten.* Grosset & Dunlap, 2001.

Yolen, Jane. *Owl Moon.* Philomel Books, 1987.

    Sleeping Ugly. Puffin, 1997.

Zemach, Margot. *It Could Always Be Worse.* Bt Bound, 1999.

Nonfiction

Sulzby, E. (1985). "Children's emergent reading of favorite storybook." *Reading Research Quarterly,* 20, 458–481.